William Harbutt Dawson

The unearned increment

Reaping without sowing

William Harbutt Dawson

The unearned increment
Reaping without sowing

ISBN/EAN: 9783744739641

Printed in Europe, USA, Canada, Australia, Japan

Cover: Foto ©ninafisch / pixelio.de

More available books at **www.hansebooks.com**

THE
UNEARNED INCREMENT:

OR,

REAPING WITHOUT SOWING.

BY

WILLIAM HARBUTT DAWSON,

AUTHOR OF "GERMAN SOCIALISM AND FERDINAND LASSALLE," "BISMARCK AND STATE SOCIALISM," ETC.

SECOND  *EDITION.*

LONDON:
SWAN SONNENSCHEIN & CO.,
PATERNOSTER SQUARE.

SOCIAL SCIENCE SERIES.
Scarlet Cloth, each 2s. 6d.

1. **Work and Wages.** Prof. J. E. THOROLD ROGERS.
   "Nothing that Professor Rogers writes can fail to be of interest to thoughtful people."—*Athenæum.*
2. **Civilisation: its Cause and Cure.** EDWARD CARPENTER.
   "No passing piece of polemics, but a permanent possession."—*Scottish Review.*
3. **Quintessence of Socialism.** Dr. SCHAFFLE.
   "Precisely the manual needed. Brief, lucid, fair, and wise."—*British Weekly.*
4. **Darwinism and Politics.** D. G. RITCHIE, M.A. (Oxon).
   NEW EDITION, with two additional Essays on HUMAN EVOLUTION.
   "One of the most suggestive books we have met with."—*Literary World.*
5. **Religion of Socialism.** E. BELFORT BAX.
6. **Ethics of Socialism.** E. BELFORT BAX.
   "Mr. Bax is by far the ablest of the English exponents of Socialism."—*Westminster Review.*
7. **The Drink Question.** Dr. KATE MITCHELL.
   "Plenty of interesting matter for reflection."—*Graphic.*
8. **Promotion of General Happiness.** Prof. M. MACMILLAN.
   "A reasoned account of the most advanced and most enlightened utilitarian doctrine in a clear and readable form."—*Scotsman.*
9. **England's Ideal, &c.** EDWARD CARPENTER.
   "The literary power is unmistakable, their freshness of style, their humour, and their enthusiasm."—*Pall Mall.*
10. **Socialism in England.** SIDNEY WEBB, LL.D.
    "The best general view of the subject from the modern Socialist side."—*Athenæum.*
11. **Prince Bismarck and State Socialism.** W. H. DAWSON.
    "A succinct, well-digested review of German social and economic legislation since 1870."—*Saturday Review.*
12. **Godwin's Political Justice (On Property).** Edited by H. S. SALT.
    "Shows Godwin at his best; with an interesting and informing Introduction."—*Glasgow Herald.*
13. **The Story of the French Revolution.** E. BELFORT BAX.
    "A trustworthy outline."—*Scotsman.*
14. **The Co-operative Commonwealth.** LAURENCE GRONLUND.
    "An independent exposition of the Socialism of the Marx School."—*Contemporary Review.*
15. **Essays and Addresses.** BERNARD BOSANQUET, M.A. (Oxon).
    "Ought to be in the hands of every student of the Nineteenth Century spirit."—*Echo.*
    "No one can complain of not being able to understand what Mr. Bosanquet means."—*Pall Mall Gazette.*
16. **Charity Organisation.** C. S. LOCH, Secretary to Charity Organisation Society.
    "A perfect little manual."—*Athenæum.*
    "Deserves a wide circulation."—*Scotsman.*

SOCIAL SCIENCE SERIES—*continued*.

17. **Thoreau's Anti-Slavery and Reform Papers.** Edited by H. S. SALT.
    "An interesting collection of essays."—*Literary World*.

18. **Self-Help a Hundred Years Ago.** G. J. HOLYOAKE.
    "Will be studied with much benefit by all who are interested in the amelioration of the condition of the poor."—*Morning Post*.

19. **The New York State Reformatory at Elmira.** ALEXANDER WINTER; with Preface by HAVELOCK ELLIS.
    "A valuable contribution to the literature of penology."—*Black and White*.

20. **Common Sense about Women.** T. W. HIGGINSON.
    "An admirable collection of papers, advocating in the most liberal spirit the emancipation of women."—*Woman's Herald*.

21. **The Unearned Increment.** W. H. DAWSON.
    "A concise but comprehensive volume."—*Echo*.

22. **Our Destiny.** LAURENCE GRONLUND.
    "A very vigorous little book, dealing with the influence of socialism on morals and religion."—*Daily Chronicle*.

23. **The Working-Class Movement in America.** Dr. EDWARD and E. MARX AVELING.
    "Will give a good idea of the condition of the working classes in America, and of the various organizations which they have formed."—*Scots Leader*.

24. **Luxury.** EMILE DE LAVELEYE.
    "An eloquent plea on moral and economical grounds for simplicity of life."—*Academy*.

25. **The Land and the Labourers.** Rev. C. W. STUBBS, M.A.
    "This admirable book should be circulated in every village in the country."—*Manchester Guardian*.

26. **The Evolution of Property.** PAUL LAFARGUE.
    "Will prove interesting and profitable to all students of economic history."—*Scotsman*.

27. **Crime and its Causes.** W. DOUGLAS MORRISON.
    "Can hardly fail to suggest to all readers several new and pregnant reflections on the subject."—*Anti-Jacobin*.

28. **Principles of State Interference.** D. G. RITCHIE, M.A.
    "An interesting contribution to the controversy on the functions of the State."—*Glasgow Herald*.

29. **German Socialism and F. Lassalle.** W. H. DAWSON.
    "As a biographical history of German socialistic movements during this century, it may be accepted as complete."—*British Weekly*.

30. **The Purse and the Conscience.** H. THOMPSON.
    "Shows common sense and fairness in his arguments."—*Scotsman*.

31. **Fustel de Coulauges' Origin of Property in Land.** Edited with a chapter on the English Manor by Prof. W. J. ASHLEY.

SWAN SONNENSCHEIN & CO., LONDON.

CONTENTS.

CHAPTER I.
Penalties of Progress 1

CHAPTER II.
Reaping without Sowing 11

CHAPTER III.
Private Gain at Public Cost 22

CHAPTER IV.
The Rent Screw 40

CHAPTER V.
The Land Monopoly 53

CHAPTER VI.
Land Speculation 62

CHAPTER VII.
Overcrowding in Large Towns 79

CHAPTER VIII.
End or Mend? 107

CHAPTER IX.
MINES AND MINERAL ROYALTIES 117

CHAPTER X.
HALF REMEDIES 127

CHAPTER XI.
ROOT AND BRANCH 140

INDEX 157

PREFACE.

Of making of books on agrarian questions there is no end. As yet, however, it cannot be said that the phase of land-law reform treated of in these pages has received the attention it deserves. "Unearned increment" is an expression which has long figured more or less prominently in the works of Liberal and Socialistic economists, both English and Continental, but it has not yet become a commonplace of polemic. If the present inquiry into the meaning and bearings of this still dignified phrase should take away something of its obscurity for the popular mind, a good purpose will certainly have been served.

It was the complaint of the elder Pliny that great estates were ruining Italy. We have in the United Kingdom a multitude of plethoric domains, and the belief is rapidly growing that their existence is not an unmixed blessing. Yet while we may run no risk, or little, of being ruined by the magnitude of individual estates, very great danger may be apprehended from the magnitude of land-values in this country, so long as, to use the words of John Stuart Mill, "an accession of wealth created by circumstances" is allowed to "become an unearned appendage to the riches of a particular class."

PREFACE.

Although writing from the English standpoint, I have not hesitated to draw illustrations of the principles advanced from various countries, particularly the United States and Germany; nor have I scrupled to borrow from abroad the testimony of political economists and social reformers favourable to those principles. The unearned increment question is, in the truest sense of the word, a social question, and if the theories advocated and the proposals recommended in these pages are vindicable as applied to one country, they may claim general validity. In endeavouring to establish the position taken up, I have sought to concentrate attention upon great principles, and in the inevitable references to persons, writing without fear or favour, I have nought extenuated while setting down nought in malice.

The annotations, which might without explanation be thought superabundant, form in reality an integral part of the plan of the work. Many facts and figures are contained therein which, though they could not properly be embodied in the text, will be found to throw important light upon the path of the uninitiated reader.

W. H. D

THE UNEARNED INCREMENT.

CHAPTER I.

PENALTIES OF PROGRESS.

IT is a fact which can need no demonstration that with the progress of society land acquires a spontaneous increase of value, a value which is independent of the expenditure of labour or money upon it. One need not be a political economist or a social reformer in order to know this. Anyone who has had occasion to work amongst ancient rent-rolls, or to trace the histories of ancient endowments in land, must often have been impressed by the vast increase which in the course of centuries has taken place in the value of landed property.[1] In former times, while this

---

[1] Here is an instance taken at random. In June, 1890, a Leeds charity case came before Mr. Justice Chitty in London, the Attorney-General applying for leave to bring in a scheme to deal with the income of the Wade Charity (Highway Trust), administered by the "Leeds Pious Uses Trustees." The testator, by will dated 1530, left certain lands whose income should "go to the use of mending the highways about Leeds." What the original value of these lands

augmentation was slow and less considerable than now, the process left all but the few unconcerned, and it was indeed seldom that serious thought was given to it. Only when the increasing value of land had produced evils of the gravest character did it become recognised that what to the majority of people seemed but a statistical curiosity, or an interesting fact in archæology, was in reality a momentous social problem.

Reliable information as to the earlier time is meagre, yet we are not left wholly in the dark. Hallam tells us in his "Europe during the Middle Ages" that arable land in England let in the thirteenth century for sixpence an acre, and meadow land for twice or thrice that sum; while from other authorities we learn that ten to fifteen years' purchase was a common estimate of value at that time. In the fifteenth century, however, land increased materially in value. Professor Thorold Rogers writes:—

"During the fifteenth century . . . notwithstanding the difficulties and losses of the landowner, the value of land rose rapidly. In the fourteenth century it was constantly obtained for ten years' purchase, the amount of land in the market being probably so abundant, and the competition for its purchase so slight, that it easily changed hands at such a rate. . . Land was valued at

---

was, I cannot learn, but in 1827 the yearly value was £627, and now it is £3,000. Again, it was stated recently, in connection with proceedings in Parliament, that the living of Burnley was a hundred years ago worth £220 annually, but the income now approximates £5,000, as the glebe land, formerly let as agricultural land, has been built upon.

twenty years' purchase in the middle of the fifteenth century. In 1469 a valuation was made of Lord Cromwell's property. His lands were estimated at a capital value of £41,940 9s. 0½d.; that is, he was considered to have a rental of £2,097 a year."[1]

Yet in the time of Henry VIII. land had a very low value when compared with modern estimates. A quarter of wheat, six sheep, or an ox would anywhere buy an acre. By the middle of the seventeenth century the rent of land had increased twenty-fold since the Middle Ages. Arthur Young estimated the rental of the agricultural land of England at £16,000,000, the average rent being 9s. 11d. per acre, against sixpence four centuries previously. At thirty years' purchase this would represent a capital value of £480,000,000.

During the last hundred years, however, the value of land in England has grown at a prodigious rate. The wars at the end of last and the beginning of the present century contributed greatly to increase rents. Sir W. Curtis declared in the House of Commons on February 17th, 1815, that "rents have in all cases doubled, and in many cases trebled, during the war." According to Mulhall, too, the land rental of

---

[1] "Six Centuries of Work and Wages," edition 1886, pp. 287, 288. Again, the same writer tells us that during the last five hundred years the rent of agricultural land has increased in England a hundred and twenty-fold when measured in money, and fourteen-fold when measured in wheat, the food of the people; but the value of building land has increased to a vastly greater extent.

the United Kingdom increased from £16,600,000 in 1750 to £23,400,000 in 1780, and £49,000,000 in 1814. But the rapid increase of population and the unparalleled development of industry have been the principal causes of the great increase in the value of land in England. According to Professor Fawcett, the capitalised value of this land now amounts to £4,500,000,000.

The income-tax returns—for whose evidence scientific accuracy cannot, it must be admitted, be claimed—testify in their own rough way to the phenomenal growth of land-values in modern times. Taking the category of land alone—which, of course, excludes the sites of buildings of all kinds—we find that the gross annual value assessed in the United Kingdom under schedule A increased from £62,000,000 in 1865 to £64,000,000 in 1869, to £67,000,000 in 1874, to £69,000,000 in 1879, and to £70,000,000 in 1880, though after that year it began steadily to fall, owing to agricultural depression and other causes. The gross annual value of messuages, tenements, &c. (in the same schedule), increased from £69,000,000 in 1865 to £80,000,000 in 1869, to £93,000,000 in 1874, to £110,000,000 in 1879, to £127,000,000 in 1884, and to £133,000,000 in 1887, the increase of £64,000,000 in twenty-two years representing far more than the increased value due to additional building. The total gross annual value of both categories, together with manors, fines, &c., increased from £132,000,000 in 1865 to £145,000,000 in 1869, to £160,000,000 in 1874, to £180,000,000 in 1879, to £190,000,000 in 1884, and to £197,000,000 in 1887.[1] Yet this increase in the value of land is not by any means peculiar to England amongst European countries. In France, Germany, and Flanders the rent and selling price of agricultural land have at least doubled within the last thirty years. According to M. de Laveleye, too, the same increase has taken place in Belgium since 1830.

[1] "It is certainly impossible," says the Hon. G. C. Brodrick in his essay on primogeniture, "to ignore the grave political danger involved in the simple fact that nearly all the soil of Great Britain, the value of which is so incalculable and progressively advancing, should belong to a section of the population relatively small and progressively dwindling. More than twenty years ago, Mr. Porter, a very high authority on economical statistics, arrived at the conclusion that, 'with scarcely any exception, the revenue drawn in the form of rent has at least doubled in every part of Great Britain since 1790.' In the period which has since elapsed the same causes have continued to operate with still greater activity. It was stated in a report issued by Mr. Goschen, as President of the Poor-law Board, that the annual value of lands, houses, railways, and other property in the United Kingdom assessed for the income tax under Schedule A, rose from £53,495,376 to £143,872,588 between 1814 and 1868 ; and this must be exclusive of the immense sums (estimated by Mr. A. Arnold at £100,000,000) received by the landed interest from railway companies over and above the market price of the land thus sold. From a later report of the Inland Revenue Office it appears that the assessment of the United Kingdom under Schedule A amounted to more than £150,000,000, and that of England and Wales alone to £122,599,255 in the year 1873-4, and the Commissioners give reasons for believing the real advance in the value of landed property to have been much greater." (*Vide* the Cobden Club's " Systems of Land Tenure in various Countries," p. 146, ed. 1881.)

But we obtain the most impressive evidence of the growth of land-value when, turning from agricultural land, we consider the land upon which towns are built. The capital value of such land has, especially in recent years, often increased to an almost incredible extent. In a city like London a square yard of a building site may now-a-days be worth as much as an acre of agricultural land. It has been calculated that the agricultural rental of the land upon which London stands would be £250,000, yet the capital value of that land, without the buildings which have been erected upon it, is placed at the enormous sum of £300,000,000. These are figures deserving meditation: £300,000,000 *for the land of London!* Contrast this sum with the value of the site of London before the shores of the Thames were covered with buildings, and we have a most remarkable, an unparalleled illustration of the growth of land-value and rent. In the City the annual value of land ordinarily reaches as high a figure as £1 10s. to £2 per square foot, equal to a capital value of £65,000 to £87,000 per acre.[1] At times, however, even this value is greatly exceeded. A land expert, giving evidence before the Select Committee who considered the Strand Improvement Bill of the London County Coun-

---

[1] See also Sir Lyon Playfair's remark at Leeds, December 13th, 1889 : " Take the case of London, spread over a vast space, which formerly was worth £3 or £4 an acre. Some parts of it are now worth from £50,000 to £60,000 in rental value."

cil, said (May 19th, 1890) he valued certain land within the area of the improvement contemplated at a minimum of £10 per square foot, equal to £90 per square yard and £435,600 per acre. Yet it is only in comparatively recent times that the bulk of this vast increase of value has accrued. "I could show," says Professor Thorold Rogers in his work on "Work and Wages," "that land for two miles round St. Paul's has increased during the last hundred and fifty years a thousandfold in value." Similarly, while land in the suburbs of Boston sells for £80,000 the acre, the rate is £160,000 in the central parts of the city.

That the rapid increase in the value of land, and with it the unexampled augmentation of rent, is a social danger, received recognition from isolated writers several centuries ago. They saw that the larger the tax claimed by the landlord for the use of the soil, the worse became the position of the cultivator and the lot of the labourer.[1] A striking passage, referring to the early part of the sixteenth century, appears in the writings of Hugh Latimer, and though often quoted it deserves repetition because of its significance :—

"Land which went heretofore for twenty or forty pounds a year now is let for fifty or a hundred. My father was a yeoman, and had no lands of his own; only, he had a farm at a rent of

---

[1] "The more there is allotted to labour the less there will remain to be appropriated as rent." (H. Fawcett, "Manual of Political Economy," p. 123.)

three or four pounds by the year at the uttermost, and thereupon he tilled so much as kept half-a-dozen men. He had walk for a hundred sheep, and my mother milked thirty kine; he was able and did find the king a harness with himself and his horse when he came to the place that he should receive the king's wages. He kept me to school; he married my sisters with five pounds apiece so that he brought them up in godliness and fear of God. He kept hospitality for his neighbours, and some alms he gave to the poor. And all this he did of the same farm where he that now hath it payeth sixteen pounds rent or more [instead of 'three or four pounds by the year at the uttermost'] by the year, and is not able to do anything for his prince, for himself, nor for his children, nor to give a cup of drink to the poor."

Ever since the time here written of rent has continued to grow, and with increasing rapidity, and as a result the social evils which are the necessary consequence of this increase of rent have tended to become acuter. The higher rent, the less the amount of income divisible between wages and interest. As the produce is distributable amongst the three factors, rent, wages, and interest, it is evident that wages and interest can only benefit by the low value of land, and that the higher land rises in value relatively the smaller will be the proportions of the produce which fall to these two factors respectively. As with the growth of population the value of land increases, it follows that the produce of labour falls more and more to the landlords, who nevertheless do nothing to deserve this augmentation of income. Society makes the land more valuable by requiring a greater area for habitable purposes and for food production, yet the increased value, instead of benefiting those who create it, injures them, proves an obstacle to their material prosperity, and is productive of innumerable social evils whose gravity it is often impossible to exaggerate.[1]

The labourer suffers in an especial degree, because, owing to the growing exactions of the landowners, the fruits of his toil have relatively an ever-diminishing value. As Mr. Henry George pertinently remarks :—

---

[1] "Not indeed that the introduction of improved processes into agriculture has been for nought; it has resulted in a large augmentation of the aggregate return obtained from the soil, but without permanently lowering its price, and therefore without permanent advantage to either capitalist or labourer, or to other consumers. The large addition to the wealth of the country has gone neither to profits nor to wages, nor yet to the public at large, but to swell a fund ever growing, even while its proprietors sleep— the rent-roll of the owners of the soil. Accordingly we find that, notwithstanding the vast progress of agricultural industry effected within a century, there is scarcely an important agricultural product that is not at least as dear now as it was a hundred years ago— as dear, not merely in money price, but in real cost. The aggregate return from the land has immensely increased ; but the cost of the costliest portion of the produce, which is that which determines the price of the whole, remains pretty nearly as it was. Profits, therefore, have not risen at all, and the real remuneration of the labourer, taking the whole field of labour, in but a slight degree— at all events in a degree very far from commensurate with the general progress of industry." (Professor J. E. Cairnes, in "Some Leading Principles of Political Economy newly Expounded," 1874, p. 333.) So Mr. A. O'Connor, M.P., observes in a minority report of the Royal Commission on Depression in Trade and Industry (1885-6) :— " Under the existing land system the owners of the soil are able to obtain, and do exact, so large a proportion of the proceeds of the industry of the United Kingdom, that the remainder is insufficient to secure adequate remuneration to the industrial classes, either in the shape of wages to operatives, or reasonable profit to the organisers of labour, the employers, or capitalists."

" Labour cannot reap the benefits which advancing civilisation brings, because they are intercepted. Land being necessary to labour, and being reduced to private ownership, every increase in the productive power of labour but increases rent—the price that labour must pay for the opportunity to realise its powers; and thus all the advantages gained by the march of progress go to the owners of the land, and wages do not increase. Wages cannot increase, for the greater the earnings of labour the greater the price that labour must pay out of its earnings for the opportunity to make any earnings at all."

Thus the Elysium of the labouring classes is not the old country where land is expensive and rent high, but the new country, where, the land monopoly not being severely felt, the proportion of the produce falling to rent is still not excessive.

" New countries, where the aggregate wealth is small, but where land is cheap, are always better countries for the labouring classes than the rich countries, where land is dear. Whereever you find land relatively low, will you not find wages relatively high? And wherever land is high, will you not find wages low? As land increases in value poverty deepens and pauperism increases. In the new settlements, where land is cheap, you will find no beggars, and the inequalities in condition are very slight. In the great cities, where land is so valuable that it is measured by the foot, you will find the extremes of poverty and of luxury, and this disparity in condition between the two extremes of the social scale may always be measured by the price of land. Land in New York is more valuable than in San Francisco, and in New York the San Franciscan may see squalor and misery that will make him stand aghast. Land is more valuable in London than in New York, and in London there is squalor and destitution worse than that of New York." [1]

---

[1] "Progress and Poverty," Book V., chapter ii.

CHAPTER II.

REAPING WITHOUT SOWING.

IN considering the increase of land-value and rent we may with advantage deal with what may, for convenience sake, be called (1) rural and (2) urban (country and town) land separately, since the causes which make for augmented value are not quite the same in both cases.

(1.) By rural land is meant purely agricultural land, land which is utilised for food production—as for the growth of corn, for grazing and pasturage, or for market gardening—or is otherwise cultivated and not built upon. Here we have to do with the alimentary needs of the population. As a community grows its greater food requirements demand the cultivation of an extended area of ground. Economic rent is, in the words of Mill, "the excess of the produce yielded by land beyond what would be returned to the same capital if employed on the worst land in cultivation." [1] It follows that the greater the area cultivated owing to the necessity for increased food supplies, the more the rent

---

[1] "Principles of Political Economy," Book II., chap. xvi., section 3.

which the owners of the soil are in a position to claim. The unoccupied land within the immediate periphery of a town is that which is first used for the production of food, and the land farther distant is put to the same use as the necessities of the population require it. As, however, the cultivators of the soil are willing to pay for convenience of access and transport, the eligible land adjacent to a town increases in value as *cultivated land*, apart from any increase from other causes. Proximity to the market, facility of transport by road, canal, or rail, increased power of production owing to such favourable position, and competition amongst tenants, are all factors which tend to augment the value of this cultivated land, and yet it will be noticed that these causes are all social. They act, as it were, automatically, and independently of the owners of the soil, who may not be responsible for any fraction of the increasing value. Thus a farm of thirty-three acres in Whalley, Derbyshire, let in 1797 for £30 a year, the landlord paying all taxes. In 1834 the same farm let for £80 a year, the taxes falling upon the tenant. Near Sandbach, Cheshire, five farms, which towards the end of last century let for £330, bore an aggregate rental of £1,720 in 1834. Again, a case is in mind where land on the outskirts of a small North of England town was let a hundred years ago at what was then regarded as the high rent of 20s. to 30s. per acre as arable land.

Now the same land, as agricultural land, brings the owners three and four times the amount, for population has grown and more food is needed there and elsewhere.[1]

There is, however, a time when the land round about towns acquires a far greater value than can be obtained so long as it is only required for food production. It is when the land ceases to be agricultural land and becomes eligible for building purposes—again a social incident which is independent of personal exertions or expenditure on the part of the owners.[2] Every large town furnishes examples in abundance of this species of value-growth. Take one which is typical.[3] Nearly fifty years ago a small estate, lying a few miles from a busy Yorkshire manufacturing town, the value of

---

[1] Compare the following candid statement:—"I once found a rent in a remote North Country dale which had not been disturbed under year to year agreements for sixty years; and when revising the rents I raised it from £28 to £82." (A Land Agent in the "Land Agents' Record" for January 4th, 1890.)

[2] A land report from Folkestone for 1889, published in an estate journal, says:—"As to the value of land from an agricultural point of view, we can say but little in its favour. The soil is of so poor a quality that its average rental value is but thirty shillings an acre. The most valuable is used for grazing purposes, principally for sheep. Once, however, let it be treated for as building land, and the value immediately assumes immense proportions, £20 a year per acre being asked for land two miles out of the town." And again:—
"Land near towns and popular centres continues to advance in value." (Buckinghamshire.)
"Lands ripe for building purposes in favourable positions, both in Leicester and the smaller towns of the county, fetch good prices and so do accommodation lands." (Leicestershire.)

[3] Related to the author by the land agent referred to.

which was £7,000, was entrusted to the management of a local land agent. From the first it was let as agricultural land, yet its value continually increased, owing to the growth of the adjacent town, and the consequent demand for eligible building land. When a few years ago the estate changed hands the value had grown from £7,000 to £50,000. The value had thus increased seven-fold in forty years, though the land was never used for other than agricultural purposes, and the landlord had done nothing whatever to improve it, having, to use the land agent's words, "had his hands in his pockets the whole time."

Where the land upon which towns are built is held by single or few persons princely incomes are frequently derived by the monopolists. Cases like those of Bury[1] (the Earl of Derby), Cardiff (the Marquis of Bute), Huddersfield (the Ramsden family), and many districts of the metropolis (the Bedford, Norfolk, Portland, and other noble families) will readily occur to those who have studied this question. In such cases it might seem as though a community only existed and pros-

---

[1] The municipal borough of Bury contains 5,835 acres, distributed as follows:—Lord Derby, 4,100 acres; glebe, 150 acres; other owners, 1,585 acres. In 1846 the rateable value was £57,608 and in 1889 it was £221,490, a quadruple increase in 43 years. It is commonly understood in Bury that Lord Derby's income from the borough is £70,000. During the last generation large blocks of property built on the 99 years' lease and three-lives' systems have "fallen in," thus adding enormously to the earl's revenue.

pered for the purpose of increasing the wealth of the landlords, for even though the latter preserved an attitude of complete passivity, their land would necessarily acquire greater value year by year. The more numerous the community becomes and the more it thrives, the higher the tribute it must pay to the owners of the soil upon which its dwellings have been placed. In lending or selling his land the owner renders now no greater service to the community than he did years ago—when land was cheaper—but he requires far greater remuneration for the service. Where the landlord, by his own labour or expenditure, increases the value of his property this growing tribute is, to some extent, justifiable; but it will generally be found that it is not the owner but society which makes the land more valuable. Nevertheless the law says that society may be rack-rented on its own improvements.

Nowhere do we find such remarkable instances of the growth of land-value as in London. The agricultural rental of the land upon which the metropolis stands has been estimated at a quarter of a million pounds, yet it is computed that its *annual rental* is between fifteen and sixteen and a half millions,[1] the difference of so many millions representing the increased value given to the land by the fact of population

---

[1] "The estimate of Mr. W. Saunders, a member of the London County Council, is £16,728,830, while Mr. Sidney Webb accepts the lower computation.

having settled upon it. A short time ago Mr. Sidney Webb made a careful estimate of the unearned increment of London, basing his calculations upon the metropolitan quinquennial valuations, and he placed the yearly addition to this increment at no less a sum than £4,500,000. The estimate was obtained in the following manner:—At the last re-valuation of the metropolitan area, in 1886, the annual rental was found to be £37,027,516, which represents a capital value of roughly £555,000,000, reckoned on fifteen years' purchase. Sixteen years before the annual rental was £22,142,706, representing a capital value of roughly £330,000,000, the gross increase for the period being in rent £14,884,810 a year, and in capital value roughly £223,000,000. The part of this increase which has resulted from building operations is approximately learned from supplementary valuations. Deducting the value thus created by the employment of capital, a balance of £6,092,680 remains as the spontaneous increase of the rental of London between the valuations of 1871 and 1886. As four quinquennial valuations have taken place during the period considered, this increase must be spread over twenty years, and this done the result is an average yearly accession of £304,634, equal to a capital value of £4,569,510. These figures demonstrate the astounding fact that during two decades the population of London has placed an additional six million pounds of rental into the landlords' pockets for no other reason than that the law allows the owners of the soil to appropriate the whole of the increment created by social causes. The capital value of this present to the landlords—reckoned on the basis of fifteen years' purchase—is no less than £91,390,200. If we assume, with Mr. Webb, that the relationship borne by the unearned increment of the last twenty years to the total increase in rental during that period applies also to the gross valuation of the metropolis (in 1886, £37,027,516), we shall have to conclude that the rent of the land upon which London stands—the "annual payment for permission merely to occupy the swampy marsh by the Thames which London labour makes so productive"—amounts to the handsome sum of fifteen million pounds yearly. Yet the agricultural value of the land cannot be more than a quarter of a million pounds, only one-sixtieth of the value which the people of London have given to it by living and toiling upon it.[1]

It would be easy to accumulate examples of the prodigious growth of land-value in and around English towns. Thus in an arbitration case which arose at Halifax during the present year a witness admitted

---

[1] The following is Mr. Webb's calculation, based on official returns:— (For Table see next page.)

having sold the Halifax Corporation four-and-a-half yards of land for £1,000, the rate being £222 a yard.[1]

On 6th April.	Gross Valuation (annual rental).	Total increase.	Increase due to new buildings (annual rental).	"Unearned increment" of annual rental.
	£	£	£	£
1870	22,142,706			
1871	24,103,083	1,960,377	*549,508	1,410,869
1872	24,388,000	284,917	284,917	—
1873	24,756,711	368,711	368,711	—
1874	25,148,033	391,322	391,322	—
1875	25,574,366	426,333	426,333	—
1876	27,602,649	2,028,283	*549,508	1,478,775
1877	28,464,833	862,184	862,184	—
1878	29,027,795	562,962	562,962	—
1879	29,682,269	654,474	654,474	—
1880	30,421,071	738,802	738,802	—
1881	33,384,851	2,963,780	*549,508	2,414,272
1882	33,855,917	471,066	471,066	—
1883	34,470,725	614,808	614,808	—
1884	35,100,704	629,979	629,979	—
1885	35,689,244	588,540	588,540	—
1886	37,027,516	1,338,282	*549,508	788,764
Average of 17 years	£29,461,204	£14,884,810	£8,792,130	£6,092,680
	Increase of 12 ordinary years	6,594,098	* Estimated at average of the other 12 years.	Average unearned increment during 20 years, £304,634
	Increase of 4 quinquennial periods	8,290,712		
	Total increase	£14,884,810		

[1] The report of the Committee on Town Holdings has a significant passage on this subject, which says:—" The decrease during the term of a 99 years' lease of the value of the fabric of a house seems, as a rule, to be accompanied by a corresponding increase in the value of the land on which it stands. And in very many cases where the landowner has received a large accession of income, the whole of the increase appears to be due to this increase of land-values; that is to say, the land, as vacant land, is

Leaving England, however, it is worth our while to look abroad, for the same startling facts confront us everywhere. "In Boston, a considerable city of 360,000 inhabitants, in the best part of the suburbs, in the fashionable residential districts, land sells at £80,000 an acre, while in the central parts of the city it sells at double that—at £160,000 an acre." In Sioux City, Iowa, which has a population of 20,000, land in the residential suburbs sold in 1887 at £4,500 the acre, and in the centre of the city at £40,000. Similarly in Salina, Kansas, a town of 8,000 people, suburban land sold at £4,500 an acre and land in the centre of the town at £30,000.[1]

Again, take the case of Berlin. Since 1865 the average value of house sites in this city—taking all dwellings and rented buildings—has increased from £2,081 to £5,700, nearly a threefold increase.[2] While

---

worth more than the land with the old house on it. Very striking evidence was given, showing that the great increase in value of the property of King Edward's School was due mainly to the large increase of ground values in the town, and that the school had derived very little benefit from the money expended by its lessees; and witnesses have spoken of the vast increases in land-values in such diverse places, amongst others, as Kingstown, Cork, Woolwich, the Portland Marylebone estate, Bethesda, and Redruth. This increase seems to be due to the situation, not to the house, or to be inherent in the land and not in the house; it is mostly position, not the outlay on the land, that gives the value."

[1] "Land Lessons from America," by Dr. A. R. Wallace (1887).

[2] "There has been an enormous rise in the value of building

the value of land has thus greatly increased, rents have proportionately risen. In 1865 the average rent was £223 9s., but it is now £571 8s.[1]

The manner in which growth of population, with corresponding increase in the demand for dwellings, leads to a rise in rents is well shown by the experience of Berlin, a case which is extremely instructive, as Berlin's growth has since 1870 been phenomenal. Statistics show that in 1878, when the demand for houses was temporarily smaller, no less than 9 per cent. of the habitable dwellings were empty, and the result was that rents fell. In that year (taking the two terms) 43,633 rents were lowered, while only 1,776 were raised. The glut of houses soon disappeared, and the percentage of empty dwellings fell in the spring term of 1886 to two. Mark the result of a greater demand. During 1886 the abatements in rent were 2,510 (against 43,633 in 1878) and the increases were 31,572 (against 1,776). The increases in rent had multiplied nearly uninterruptedly since 1878, as the following figures show:—April 1, 1878, 846; October 1, 930;

---

land at Berlin. A plot of ground in the Müllerstrasse, which was purchased in 1855 for £500, is now valued at £150,000, and the owner has refused an offer of £100,000 for it."—*Newspapers for September,* 1890.

[1] According to a return recently laid before the Union of Berlin Landowners' Associations, the German metropolis had in 1889 22,400 houses with 385,000 dwellings, representing a value of 5,321,000,000 marks (*circa* £266,000,000), with aggregate rent of 256,000,000 marks (£12,800,000).

April, 1879, 867; October, 1,024; April, 1880, 1,568; October, 1,820; April, 1881, 3,011; October, 3,642; April, 1882, 3,160; October, 3,119; April, 1883, 3,344; October, 4,775; April, 1884, 4,978; October, 8,452; April, 1885, 11,062; October, 14,956; April, 1886, 14,533; October, 17,039; April, 1887, 18,422. Later statistics are not available. During this decennial period the population had increased some three hundred thousand.

CHAPTER III.

PRIVATE GAIN AT PUBLIC COST.

IF we take the second class of land, urban land, we find that the causes of the increase in value are in part different, while also more active and effectual. Urban land, the land which is covered by buildings, or which may prospectively be so utilised, acquires greater value from (1) the mere growth of the community—city, town, or village, as the case may be; (2) from the carrying out of public improvements; and (3) from the enterprise and exertions of the individual residents. And here again the landowner may play an absolutely passive part.

(1.) *Growth of population.*—The progress of a community in numbers and wealth will of necessity increase the value of the land occupied, and, therefore, the income or rent which falls to those who own the land upon and near which the population dwells. The greater the demand for land for building purposes, the greater the competition for houses, the better the dwellings tenanted, and the higher will be the landlords' rent and the higher the price of land. A remarkable case of value-creation by the mere settlement of population upon the land was related in the House of Commons on May 6th, 1890, by Colonel Hughes.

"In the parish of Plumstead land used to be let for agricultural purposes for £3 an acre. The income of an estate of 250 acres in 1845 was £750 per annum, and the capital value at twenty years' purchase was £15,000. The arsenal came to Woolwich; with the arsenal the necessity for 5,000 houses. And then came the harvest for the landlord. The land, the capital value of which had been £15,000, now brought an income of £14,250 per annum. The ground landlord has received £1,000,000 in ground rents already, and after twenty years hence the Woolwich estates, with all the houses upon them, will revert to the landowner's family—bringing another million—meaning altogether a swap of £15,000 for a sum of £2,000,000."

To take an illustration from Ireland. Giving evidence before the Select Committee on Town Holdings, Captain Richard O'Sullivan said:—

"Queenstown in the course of a century has grown by the sheer industry and enterprise of its inhabitants from a barren rock into a property valued at £21,000 a year, a value for a lump sum equivalent to half-a-million pounds. None of it has been created by the landlord, yet he tries to confiscate it. Nearly eight miles of roads and streets, with their flagged footways, main sewers, private drainage, crossings, channels, &c., costing at least £30,000, have been paid for out of the pockets of the people, and on the expiration of the leases the landlord confiscates them also. The public quays have been built at the public expense, and even the foreshore upon which they are erected had after great and expensive litigation to be paid for to the utmost farthing to the landlords, who refused to contribute in the smallest degree to the erection of the quays. The town as it stands has been paid for many times over by the occupiers, and yet the landlords claim it as their own, and except the occupiers are prepared to purchase it over again at a fabulous amount they must clear out and leave the labour of their lives to the landlords, if the Government fails to give them protection."

Another witness in the same inquiry, Mr. Beveridge, said of Dublin, that a considerable increase in the value of land had taken place there, this being " due in great measure to the growth of population." Asked, " Is it due to any action on the part of the landlords—the persons who own this land ? " he replied : " There may be individual cases in which a landlord has effected improvements, but I do not know of any." Again, he stated : " The general improvement of the land in Dublin is, in my opinion, attributable mainly to two causes. The first is, the growth of the population in the city. The second is, the enormous expenditure that has been made on new roadways, good sewers, water supply, and so on."

(2.) *Public Improvements.*—These, too, tend to increase the value of urban property. In the category of public improvements fall all the permanent works carried out by local authorities at the expense of the ratepayers in the interest of the latter's convenience and health ; such are roads, bridges, public buildings, parks and open spaces in large towns, sewerage, lighting, water supply, &c. The cost of these works—where, as in the case of water and gas, private enterprise does not step in—is a common charge on the inhabitants.[1] It is true that these benefit by improvements of the kind, but they are not the only or the principal ones to benefit. The house occupiers only have a temporary interest in the public works constructed at their expense, and they of necessity renounce that interest directly they change their abode. But there is a class of men whose benefit from public works is permanent, though they do not to any considerable extent, if at all, contribute towards the cost. These are the owners of the land upon which the town stands, for though it might at first sight seem as though the inhabited buildings increased in value as a consequence of public improvements, the augmented value falls in reality to the land they cover

[1] "As a matter of fact," writes Professor Thorold Rogers, in his work, "Six Centuries of Work and Wages" (ed. 1886, p. 533), "the owner contributes nothing to local taxation. Everything is heaped on the occupier. The land would be worthless without roads, and the occupier has to construct, widen, and repair them. It could not be inhabited without proper drainage, and the occupier is constrained to construct and pay for the works which give an initial value to the ground rent, and, after the outlay, enhance it. It could not be occupied without a proper supply of water, and the cost of this supply is levied on the occupier also. In return for the enormous expenditure paid by the tenant for these permanent improvements, he has his rent raised on his improvements, and his taxes increased by them. The occupier in towns is worse used by far than the Irish tenant was before the changes of the Land Act, for if the landlord made him pay interest on his own outlay the cost of local taxation was shared between the parties."

and adjoin.¹ If any one doubts whether the works alluded to increase the value of property, and are essential to the maintenance of value, let him imagine what would be the effect of their absence upon the property which now they benefit.² Let a local authority, for example, be supposed to divert its attention from one quarter of a town to another. In one place the roads are allowed to fall into decay; sanitation is neglected—the streets are unclean, the draining of the houses is deficient, the water supply is faulty; public convenience is no longer regarded—no more thoroughfares are widened, no more old buildings are removed. All these acts of omission and commission on the part of the local authority will tend to depreciate the value of the property thus neglected, while the parts of the town to which attention is transferred will proportionately increase in value. It is evident, therefore, that the value of urban land is at once preserved and augmented by the public improvements which are

---

[1] In the United States this is widely recognised by law and custom. Thus the Muncipal Code of Ohio says:—"An assessment for the construction of sewers is in its nature a charge for a permanent addition to the freehold, and is to be paid by *the owner of the fee or the holder of a perpetual lease,* but is not chargeable against an ordinary tenant for years."

[2] Note the following extract from a land report for 1889:—"In Portsmouth, large numbers of small houses have been erected, and land development has been fairly brisk. Where roads have been made up, curbed, channelled, and drained, £1,200 to £1,600 per acre has been readily obtained on estates skirting the populous parts of the town."

carried out at the expense, not of the owners of that property, but of the residents who have only a temporary interest in it. Further, we are confronted with the singular anomaly that the community which in this way gives to the property it uses a higher value, actually pays the landlords for the privilege of creating that higher value for them. For the more valuable urban property becomes, owing to the growth of population, public improvements, and other social causes, the higher become also the rents which are demanded of the occupiers.

This second factor in the creation of increased value is the more important at the present time because the tendency of local authorities is to embark more and more boldly upon works of public utility of the kind named. Never before were communities so alive to the importance of careful sanitation; never before did they pay so much regard to their own physical welfare—as evidenced by the provision of spacious streets, public parks and open spaces; never before did they devote so much attention to the intellectual and æsthetical sides of social and civil life, in proof of which the public museums, galleries, libraries, and schools established in such abundance all over the country may be mentioned. Almost invariably the great expenditure incurred by works of these kinds has a tendency to increase the desirability of the towns concerned as places of residence, to promote the material progress of the inhabitants, and thus to augment the value of the land upon which the inhabitants are settled.[1]

A few figures, by way of illustration, will make clear to us the extent to which local taxation is employed in the execution of public improvements which make for greater land-value and higher rent. The aggregate amount of the local budgets of England and Wales for the year 1885-6 was £55,738,420 (a good deal more than half the imperial revenue), of which sum £32,177,883 was levied by rates, though a little more than forty years ago the sum raised in rates was only £8,550,000.[2] This enormous taxation includes, of course, the interest payable on public loans, the amount

---

[1] Giving evidence before the Parliamentary Committee which a short time ago considered the Liverpool Extension Bill, Mr. Shelmerdine, the City Surveyor, referred to the purchase of Sefton Park as follows:—"With regard to Sefton Park, there could be no shadow of a doubt that the construction of that park had developed the estates in the immediate neighbourhood. The agricultural value of the land to Lord Sefton was £1,350. Lord Sefton got £250,000 from the Corporation, which, at 4 per cent., would give his lordship a return of £10,000, which was a very good thing for him. The park had been of enormous benefit to Lord Sefton in developing the land around. No doubt the land around would have been developed sooner or later, but he maintained that it was developed quicker, and the class of residents were much better than his lordship would probably have got had the park not been there. Thus, in addition to the £250,000, he had for twenty-three years got this increased income from the accelerated development of his land. The portion of Lord Sefton's land still undisposed of was very small."

[2] These figures are taken from Mr. J. F. Moulton's little work on "The Taxation of Ground Values."

of which several years ago was no less than a hundred and sixty millions. As these loans are only contracted on permanent improvements, it is safe to say that the value of property has increased, or will increase, by every pound spent and borrowed by local authorities. London alone has incurred a debt of something like £40,000,000 on account of public improvements, the effect of which has generally been to make the land on which London stands more valuable.[1] The report of the Committee on Town Holdings says :—

"In the metropolis the gross debt of the late Metropolitan Board of Works outstanding on the 31st December, 1887, amounted to £27,834,000, expended entirely on works of a permanent character. The charges levied in the form of local rates to meet this liability have been paid entirely by the occupiers of the metropolis, but it is important to note that this contributes in many cases to increase the value of the premises which revert to the landlord at the end of a lease there or in any part of the country where similar conditions prevail." [2]

---

[1] Speaking in the Memorial Hall, July 29th, 1887, Mr. Gladstone alluded to the Thames Embankment, and asked, "At w ose expense was that great, permanent, and stable improvement made? Instead of being made, as it should have been, at the expense of the permanent proprietary interests, it was charged, every shilling of it, upon occupants, that is to say, mainly either upon the wages of the labouring man, in fuel necessary for his family, or upon the trade and industry and enterprise which belong of necessity to a vast metropolis like this."
[2] Sir C. Russell, Q.C., M.P., stated at a public meeting held in St. James's Hall, London, February 14th, 1889, to consider the question of the better housing of the industrial classes, that "the occupying classes of London bore a payment of £800,000 a year in recoupment of money borrowed for great improvements, the benefit of which had gone to enhance the value of the property of the landlords; and yet towards this taxation the landowners contributed nothing."

That the anomalies under consideration have not escaped the attention of German economists may be seen from the writings of Professor A. Wagner, of Berlin; take the following passage:—

"The great expenditure of the State, and particularly of the community—out of the resources of the entire population, and, with increasing taxation and its effects, for the most part out of the resources of those who do not own land—for streets, cleanliness, sanitation, security, education, &c., has ultimately the tendency to increase the height of *rente* and the value of property in urban land and buildings, because the increase of the urban population is thereby favoured. In such cases the urban landowner profits doubly, and the land-less population pays in taxes the money for expenditure which indirectly leads to a new increase in rents, thus suffering in two ways."[1]

It is impossible, of course, to say exactly to what extent the value of land in large towns is increased by the fact of population growing, and to what extent by public improvements. Yet valuable data were placed before the Select Committee which recently considered the Strand Improvement Bill of the London County Council.[2] The promoters of this measure instanced the following among other cases where property had

---

[1] "Allgemeine oder theoretische Volkswirthschaftslehre," 1st part, "Grundlegung," pp. 658, 659.

[2] During the hearing of evidence it was proved that owners of property adjoining the projected improvement of the Strand had bound leasehold tenants to agree to an increase in rent in the event of the improvement being carried out. The following advertisement, showing how public improvements are speculated upon, was read:—"*Strand.*—One door from Newcastle Street. Freehold premises situate Nos. 4 and 5 and 6, Stanhope Market,

increased in value after street improvements had been executed, and yet no structural alterations had taken place :—

	Date of improvement.	Assessment before improvement.	Assessment after improvement.			Increased value since improvement.
			1875	1880	1885	
		£	£	£	£	£
A	1871	755	806	1,250	1,250	490
B	,,	925	1,300	1,300	1,300	375
C	,,	760	1,100	1,030	1,030	270
D	,,	440	700	700	700	260
E	,,	570	900	900	900	330
F	,,	400	600	600	600	200
A	1875	48	...	60	110	62
B	,,	60	...	80	120	60
A	1876	72	...	72	120	48
B	,,	75	...	100	105	30
C	,,	200	...	240	240	40
A	1877	100	...	120	220	120
B	,,	90	...	150	150	60
C	,,	72	...	150	150	78
D	,,	60	...	120	96	36
A	1878	54	...	100	100	46
B	,,	64	...	100	100	36
C	,,	75	...	75	120	45
D	,,	100	...	100	168	68
E	,,	160	...	170	210	50
F	,,	126	...	165	165	39
G	,,	90	...	112	170	80
H	,,	70	...	100	150	80
I	,,	106	...	106	260	154
J	,,	40	...	50	105	65
K	,,	120	...	155	200	80
A	1884	1,000	...	...	1,500	500
B	,,	1,080	...	...	1,800	720
C	,,	180	...	...	250	70
D	,,	3,000	...	...	3,600	600

Stanhope Street, Clare Market, with the dwelling-houses and workshops in the rear, occupying an area of about 2,900 superficial feet, at present let and producing about £340 a year, *with the prospect of considerably enhanced value upon contemplated extensive improvements in the vicinity being carried out.*"

During the consideration of the same Bill it was stated by an official valuer (May 16th, 1890) that the rateable value of the property within the area covered by this measure had risen from £54,159 in 1856 (when the Metropolitan Board of Works began to carry out street improvements) to £147,986 in 1889. From 1865 to 1875 the increase was £42,648, and from 1875 to 1885 it was £35,505. In this district the percentage of increase during the period named had been 173·34, the percentage for the whole metropolis being 175. Asked, "To what do you attribute the rise in the rateable value in this district?" witness replied, "Chiefly to the opening of the Law Courts and the general expansion of the value of property in the metropolis."[1]

Pepys, in his famous "Diary" (date December 3rd, 1667), tells how the value of land in London rose after the Great Fire. Speaking of the new street that is to be made from Guildhall down to Cheapside," he instances the case of one owner "who hath a piece of ground lying in the very middle of the street that must be, which, when the street is out out of it, there will remain ground enough on each side to build a house to front the street. He demanded £700 for the ground, and to be excused paying anything for the melioration of the rest of his ground that he was to keep. The Court consented to give him £700, only not to abate him the consideration which the man desired ; but told them, and so they agreed, that he would excuse the City the £700, that he might have the benefit of the melioration without paying anything for it. So much some will get by having the City burned. Ground, by this means, that was not worth 4d. a foot before, will now, when houses are built, be worth 15s. a foot. But he [Sir Richard Ford] tells me of the common standard now reckoned on between man and man in places where there is no alteration of circumstances, but only the houses burnt ; there the ground which with a house on it

It is not necessary, however, to restrict ourselves to London. Other large towns have also expended enormous sums in public improvements, with the same result.[1] Take the case of Birmingham, which is a typical illustration of the growth of land-value owing to social causes of the kind under consideration. The industrial and commercial energy and enterprise of this city are famous throughout the world. The prosperity of Birmingham has been built up by the pluck, the skill, and the enlightenment of its citizens. At the beginning of the century the population only numbered 60,000, but this number is now exceeded by 400,000, a phenomenal increase due to the industrial and mercantile development, and the existence of an unusually intelligent and vigorous municipal life. Birmingham has distinguished itself among the great cities and towns of England by public spiritedness and liberality in all matters affecting the health and enlightenment of its inhabitants, and herein is a very important factor in its progress and prosperity. It was stated at a recent meeting of the City Council, in the course of

---

did yield £100 a year is now reputed worth £33 6s. 8d., and that this is the common market price between one man and another made upon a good and moderate medium."

[1] In an arbitration case which arose at Halifax this year, owing to the local Corporation requiring two properties belonging to a tradesman for the purpose of public improvements, £14,850 was claimed for premises which between 1874 and 1878 were purchased for £5,700, to which £2,000 must be added for later improvements; a total of £7,700, or just half the sum demanded.

D

a debate on the subject of taxing ground rents, that the ratepayers had expended £700,000 in sewerage works alone, that a further £300,000 had been spent on the improvement of the streets, and that other improvement schemes in progress would increase the capital expenditure on public works to over a million and a half.[1] What has been the effect on the value of property? The same authority stated that the unearned increment created in Birmingham during the fifteen years preceding 1885 was £127,000 (the increase in the annual value having been from £1,065,000 to £1,192,000, after making allowance for new buildings and other deductions), representing a capital value, at fifteen years' purchase, of £1,905,000; and at twenty years' purchase, one of £2,540,000. The yearly increase in the rental value of the land on which Birmingham stands he placed at £8,500, equal to a capital value of £127,500 or £170,000, according as the basis of calculation is fifteen or twenty years' purchase. Mr. Fulford said that "The increase in the value of land in Birmingham in recent years had been enormous. If he went back thirty or fifty years he could point to the estate of Lord Calthorpe, consisting of about 2,000 acres, the intrinsic value of which was about as many pounds per annum, but which was now

---

[1] Speech of Councillor Fulford, meeting of February 18th, 1890.

worth fifty or a hundred times as much." "The enormous value of the land," he added, "had not accrued from the labour or capital of those who owned it. It was the effect of the growth of the population, and of the great commerce and industry which the enterprise of the population had created. Another cause was the public expenditure in maintaining and increasing the value of the landowners' property, for the development of Birmingham would have been impossible if the expenditure had not been incurred."

It is well for the ratepayers of England that the exemption of the land from local taxation has become a burning question, upon which both political parties are often to be found united. In Parliament itself voices were long ago raised in favour of reform. The Select Committee of the House of Commons which in 1866 reported on the Local Government and Local Taxation of London, recognising the fact that "nearly the whole of the expenditure and obligations of the Metropolitan Board of Works had been incurred for the purpose of supplying the wants arising from the defects of former administration of the metropolis, and of effecting permanent improvements, which have tended to increase the value of property, and that the effect of works of such magnitude will be felt long after all the charges have been defrayed," recommended unanimously, " That in any arrangement of the financial resources of the Metropolitan Board, a portion of the charges for permanent improvements and works should be borne by the *owners of property* within the metropolis, the rate being, in the first instance, paid by the occupier, and subsequently deducted from his rent, as is now provided in regard to the general property tax." Encouraged by this recommendation the Corporation of London promoted a Bill the following year empowering them to levy a tax of sixpence in the pound on owners of property within the City on behalf of improvements to be executed therein. This Bill was considered by the Select Committee, which regarded it as too far-going. Nothing has been done from that day to this.

Again, the report of Mr. Goschen's Select Committee on Local Taxation, which met in 1870, declared the conviction of all members, for the report was adopted unanimously, "That the existing system of local taxation, under which the exclusive charge of almost all rates leviable upon rateable property for current expenditure, as well as for new objects and permanent works, is placed by law upon the occupiers, while the owners are generally exempt from any direct or immediate contributions in respect of such rates, is contrary to sound policy . . . [and] . . . that it is expedient to make owners as well as occupiers directly liable for a certain proportion of the rates."

Many years later, as nothing had meantime been

done, Mr. W. Saunders moved in the House of Commons (March 16th, 1886), the following resolution :—
"That no system of taxation can be equitable unless a direct assessment be imposed on the owners of ground rents, and on the owners of increased values imparted to lands by building operations or other improvements, as recommended by the Royal Commission on the Housing of the Working Classes."[1] The resolution was referred to the Select Committee on Town Holdings, and the question was again shelved.

Reform in local taxation will, no doubt, be accelerated

---

[1] Compare Mill:—"It is only in exceptional cases, like that of favourite situations in large towns, that the predominant element in the rent is the ground rent : and among the very few kinds of income which are fit subjects for peculiar taxation, these ground rents hold the principal place, being the most gigantic example extant of enormous accessions of riches acquired rapidly, and in many cases unexpectedly, by a few families, from the mere accident of their possessing certain tracts of land, without their having themselves aided in the acquisition by the smallest exertion, outlay, or risk. So far, therefore, as a house-tax falls on the ground landlord, it is liable to no valid objection." ("Political Economy," Book V., chap. iii., sec. 6.)

But an earlier advocate of such special taxation may be found in Adam Smith himself, who writes :—"Both ground rents and the ordinary rent of land are a species of revenue which the owner in many cases enjoys without care or attention of his own. Though a part of this revenue should be taken from him in order to defray the expenses of the State, no discouragement will thereby be given to any sort of industry. The annual produce of the land and labour of society, the real wealth and revenue of the great body of the people, might be the same after such a tax as before. Ground rents and the ordinary rent of land are, therefore, perhaps the species of revenue which can best bear to have a peculiar tax imposed upon them. Ground rents seem, in this respect, a more proper subject of peculiar taxation than even the ordinary rent of land. The ordinary rent of land is

by the agitation which has of late sprung up in the country. Manchester is one of the important towns where an urgent demand has been made for the taxation of ground rents, and not long ago the City Council adopted unanimously a resolution expressing "its sense of the great anomaly that arises from the entire exemption of the ground landlords from any liability towards the relief of local taxation," and considering that "the time has fully arrived when all ground or chief rents, freeholds, and mineral royalties should contribute their equitable share on the same ratio as house and other properties towards the financial burdens of the communities." It was stated in the course of the debate that "although houses and buildings of every description were rated to the extent of 4s. 2d. in the pound on the assessment, the ground landlord took in many cases *one hundred-fold the*

---

in many cases, owing partly at least to the attention and good management of the landlord. A very heavy tax might discourage too much this attention and good management. Ground rents, so far as they exceed the ordinary rent of land, are altogether owing to the good government of the Sovereign, which, by protecting the industry either of the whole people, or of the inhabitants of some particular place, enables them to pay so much more than its real value for the ground which they build their houses upon, or to make to its owner so much more than compensation for the loss which he might sustain by this use of it. Nothing can be more reasonable than that a fund which owes its existence to the good government of the State should be taxed peculiarly, or should contribute something more than the greater part of other funds towards the support of that government." ("Wealth of Nations," Book V., chapter ii, part ii., article 1, section on "Taxes upon the Rents of Houses.")

original value of the land and paid no local rates whatever."

The injustice of the present arrangement is well illustrated by the experience of Bury at the present time. The land on which this large Lancashire town stands belongs to Lord Derby, yet the *ratepayers* have been called upon to carry out sewage works (for the purpose of keeping the river Irwell pure) which would cost £60,000. As these works benefit the landlord equally with the residents, the latter have declined to execute them until the cost can be fairly divided. A town's meeting on June 3rd, 1890, passed a resolution desiring the Town Council not to proceed until—"having regard to the assurance given to the House of Commons on the 18th July, 1888, by the Right Hon. W. H. Smith, First Lord of the Treasury, in perfect good faith and with absolute sincerity, that it was the intention of the Government to deal with the question of rating at the earliest possible moment"—Parliament "has found opportunity to deal with the question of rating, and to provide a more equitable mode of raising the money required for the construction and maintenance of this great permanent public improvement."

CHAPTER IV.

THE RENT SCREW.

THEN, again, the enterprise and business skill of a town's residents produce the same effect of increasing the value of the land upon which the town stands. The high reputation of a single tradesman may improve all the property surrounding that which he occupies; while the fact of a prosperous industry or trade becoming located in a town or a certain quarter of a town may add enormously to the landlords' revenue. This accident of favourable locality is, indeed, a matter of the utmost importance in large towns.[1]

---

[1] Mr. B. F. C. Costelloe, a member of the London County Council, wrote in the *Star* of London, in January, 1890:— "I am impressed by the fact that the popularity of the cry for leasehold reform is greatly due to the general conviction that the shopkeepers and small tradesfolk are systematically despoiled by the landlord whenever a lease falls in. The freeholder, or a long lessee, lets a foothold in the business life of London to an industrious and enterprising trader—a butcher, a photographer, a grocer, a printer, a draper, what you will. The working occupier gets a lease for a few years, puts in what needful capital he can raise, spends freely his own time and brains, and 'makes a business.' But that business is often wholly and always partially annexed to the spot where it is made. There are not a dozen bakers in London who would not pay a heavy fine rather than move a mile. Therefore, you have him in a trap. Some security you must offer him,

THE RENT SCREW. 41

Evidence of indefinite extent might be adduced to show that both in large and small towns, though especially in the former, occupiers of property frequently suffer great injustice and hardship at the hands of landlords who are enriched by their energy, industry, and enterprise. In London, for example, recent agitations and consequent revelations have established the existence of infamous rack-renting as a result of the prodigious value to which land has there been forced up. The "bitter cry" of the Tenant Tradesmen's National Union[1] and the Fair Rent League, both

---

or he will not put his money down. But the competition is keen, and he will take a wonderfully short tenure. That done, you watch his business with affectionate interest, for you will skim the cream off it by-and-by. Knowing he cannot leave without a loss of, say £1,000, you will fine him £900 for your leave to stay. You first charge him what you like for 'dilapidation' so called; then you lay on a rent probably beyond what another man would give you; then you ask a fine in cash or in the form of building improvements, remembering all the while that amazing axiom of the law, that whatever of his property he affixes to the soil forthwith belongs to you."

[1] The programme of the Tenant Tradesmen's National Union lays down the following among other objects:—"To oppose generally the exactions of unjust landlords; to secure to the tenant tradesman the full value of the goodwill which he has created or purchased; to secure to the tenant the value of permanent improvements made by him during his tenancy." A news report which appeared in the *Pall Mall Gazette* in January, 1890, is, to say the least, significant:—"Last night a company of London rack-rented tradesmen met in conference at Exeter Hall. The speakers hailed from all districts of London, and the meeting was unanimous in its condemnation of the law which permitted landlords to extort arbitrary rents. If rack-rented, the speakers were not robbed of their forcefulness of expression. 'Slaves,' said one speaker, 'I should think we are, only we pay our slave-owners.' It was shown that the more successful a tradesman proved himself

formed in the metropolis in 1889, is that impossible rents are demanded in wealthy and poor neighbourhoods alike.[1]

Leaseholders suffer severely under the system which gives to the landowner all the unearned increment created by the community. As the law now stands,

---

the more was he fleeeed because of his success, and instances were given of the exorbitant rates tenants paid in comparison to those levied on the ground landlords. Another speaker exclaimed of the landlords, 'Bring them forward before us, and if they escape may heaven help them'; and then he appealed to the audience to join the Tradesmen's Union. The following resolutions were carried with enthusiasm:—'That this meeting condemns the system by which the arbitrary exactions of unjust landlords are legalised; that this meeting pledges itself to support the Tenant Tradesmen's National Union in its efforts to secure to tenants the value of the goodwill which they have created, and of all permanent improvements that they have made at their own cost.'"

[1] In May, 1890, the London newspapers recorded the formation of a Fair Rent Union, with the object of "sweeping away the slums and all other unsanitary structures," and of uniting in "a demand for the extension of the principle of judicial rents to town and country."

A passage from a letter written to the *Times* in November, 1889, by Lieut.-Col. G. H. Lloyd-Verney, who styled himself "a ground landlord on a small scale in London," seems to show that the tenants have reason for dissatisfaction. "I venture to think," he says, "if landlords in London took as much interest in and were as easily accessible to their tenants as they are in the country the relations between landlord and tenant would be less strained; but many landlords in London leave the whole of the administration of their properties in the hands of agents, who are often paid by a percentage on the rents obtained, and to whom the rack-renting of tenants is a decided advantage. Few tenants in London have the same access to their landlords that tenants have in the country, and can only approach the landlord through his agent, who, though perhaps a sharp man of business, thinks more of his own percentage and endeavours to squeeze all he can out of the tenant than to accept an equitable rent and promote harmony and kindly feeling between landlord and tenant."

not only is society as a whole unable to share in the increasing value which it gives to the land it uses, but the individual citizen is debarred from compensation for the improvements he may have made to the property he occupies. Worse than that, it is in the power of the landlord—and the power is not ignored—to make tenants' improvements a pretext for demanding additional rent.

Indeed, so far is this practice of exploitation carried, that often where a tenant has established a business which cannot easily be removed, whose success is dependent on local circumstances, the landlord converts his prerogative of changing tenants into a weapon for enforcing higher rent.[1] The Select Committee on Town Holdings has reported :—

---

[1] The following is from a daily newspaper (1889) :—" As an illustration of what a London landlord can exact I may quote the case of a well-known and most prosperous theatrical manager. He now pays £10,000 a year for his theatre. The rent has been steadily raised for years, till it is more than double the original amount, though the lessee has spent £30,000 in improvements. If he were to quit, the landlord would probably not get a tenant, certainly not at such a rental. But the manager cannot quit, because no other theatre would suit him as well."
The following passage from Adolph Wagner's work on the "Theory of Political Economy" (his *Grundlegung*, Leipzig, various editions) given us the views on this question of one of the foremost political economists of Germany :—" A still unfrequented quarter of a town, with new houses, or hitherto either without retail businesses or without good ones, is improved by the owners of the latter. But the fruits of individual industry—which often are very considerable—and even of the expenditure of capital are only enjoyed by the shopkeeper during the first period of his leasehold. Afterwards he must hand them over to the landlord either wholly

"Numerous cases have been laid before the Committee where it has been alleged that greater injustice has been done to tenants who have expended large sums in improvements by their having, at the termination of their leases, either to give up the property so improved without any compensation for the improvements made, or to pay an increased rent for the premises in consequence of the improvements made at their own expense. Somewhat similar grievances are alleged to exist in relation to the tenant's goodwill. This is said in many cases to be practically confiscated by the landlord, who takes advantage of the fact of the tenant having worked up a good business, in order to obtain on a renewal of the lease a rent higher than the market value, and that the tenant is induced to pay such rent in consequence of the great injury that would ensue to his business if he had to quit."

Again, we may read in the same report :—

"There is a widely-spread sense of injustice among lessees in having, at the end of the lease, to give up the buildings they have erected, or to pay a rent calculated on the principle that such buildings are the property of the landlord. This feeling is pro-

---

or in part in the form of increased rent—so easy to enforce—and in any case he must divide them with him. From henceforth the shopkeeper works and struggles essentially for *him*—a far more unfavourable economic relationship than the feudal burdening of the peasantry with services and dues to the landowner in the middle ages. For those burdens might not be increased at will, and if the peasant did his duty he could not be driven away. But the shopkeeper in a large town is continually being more encumbered, and may be immediately driven away, and must ever suffer from the often so dishonest competition of his rivals—this being, too, an effect of the rent-screw—everything tending ultimately to the increase of the landlord's income. He is not, indeed, bound to the soil, he is ' personally free '; that is, he can go when his lease expires, and—begin again from the beginning. In such cases, which are typical of retail businesses in large towns, because their customers are essentially *local*, and which might be instanced in hundreds, it is clear that private property in land and houses can lead to an economic exploitation which is not often reached in unfreedom." (See note to page 656.)

bably especially strong in cases where working men and others build their own houses, and where, being unable to obtain land either as freehold or long leasehold, they are practically compelled to build on leases for short terms. A good deal of evidence has been laid before us as to places where these conditions exist, such as the quarry districts of Festiniog and Bethesda, and the mining districts of Cornwall, where large numbers of houses are built by workmen for their own occupation on land previously of little or no value, and where, in many cases, the whole labour and expense of preparing the site, erecting the house, and all other outlay on the property is paid by the lessee. It cannot be a matter of surprise that such a lessee should feel that he is unjustly treated under a system which gives the value of the building and improvements to the lessor at the expiration of a term, in many cases, comparatively short."[1]

In regard to the complaints of rack-renting upon tenants' improvements, the Committee—while not justifying them generally—reported that it was of opinion that—

"As a rule, any improvements which may have been made by the tenant are regarded as the rightful property of the landlord on the termination of the lease, and that in such cases rents are commonly raised in consequence of such improvements to the extent of either a part or the whole of the increased value they may have given to the premises."

And, again—

"It cannot be doubted that cases of hardship do occur in con-

---

[1] Captain R. O'Sullivan stated before the Committee that he leased a house site in an Irish town for 20 years at £3 17s. per annum, building a residence which cost £400. On the expiration of the lease the structure went to the landlord, to whom the builder had in future the pleasure of paying £10 a year rent for his own house.

nection with goodwill, and that landlords sometimes take an undue advantage of their tenants' position in such cases; and it is clear that when the renewal of a lease of business premises is under discussion, the fact of the tenant having created a valuable goodwill gives the landlord considerable power to settle the terms of such renewal in his own favour." [1]

The Committee did not, save in exceptional cases, recommend the compensation of tenants under existing contracts for improvements or goodwill on the termination of their tenancies, but as to future contracts they felt that "No injustice would be involved in such an alteration of the law as would entitle the tenant of trade or business premises, on the expiration of his tenancy, to compensation for such improvements as he may have *bona fide* made for the purpose of carrying on his trade or business, and as may have added to the permanent letting value of the premises."

---

[1] One witness declared: "The tenants are not considered at all now in a renewal; they are simply told by the agents, no matter whom they represent, that they must pay just such a full price as they could get from any stranger outside. Of course, the tenant in possession, who has spent a lot of money in making a goodwill, is bound to pay more than anyone else, and a stranger will pay a higher price for the sake of getting the goodwill of the business that the other man has made." Another witness said that "the landlords do in a large number of instances trade upon the special interest a man has in his lease," and yet another "showed that in his own case he had been obliged to pay as heavily for the business he had established as its profits would allow of by way of increase of rent." The Committee's report adds to these statements: "The general answer of the land agents to these complaints was, that when a tenant takes up a lease he does it with his eyes open to the risks of being either turned out or being forced to pay an increased rent at the end of the term."

The Committee reported to the same effect regarding Ireland :—

"There is no doubt that a constant increase of rent is made on the tenants' improvements in most of the towns of Ireland; and that the circumstance of their possessing a goodwill is an important factor to induce the tenants to accede to such a rise. In many cases the grievance does not arise from the action of the ground landlord, but from that of the middleman. It is difficult to devise any fair remedy for such a state of things, but the Committee are of opinion that a considerable number of hardships arise owing to the short tenures on which houses have been built, and substantial improvements effected, in many of the Irish towns, although this is being to some extent remedied, either by the influence of public opinion, or by landlords seeing that it is for their interest to grant longer terms."

It would be easy to multiply evidence of the evils of urban landlordism when combined with the power of appropriating the whole of the socially-created value of land. The very existence of such a power will always be a social danger, for land being a monopoly article, society is, beyond the limits within which the rights and privileges of the monopolists are restricted, absolutely at the mercy of the owners of the soil, whose demands upon the material resources of the community are often not even limited by the latter's ability to respond. Take the following instance of a landlord's power being asserted to the direct injury of society. The Committee on Town Holdings reports :—

"Mr. Burr gave some most unpleasantly cynical evidence to the effect that, in the course of his individual management of leasehold estates at Wimbledon, Torquay, and Swansea, he systematically worked the covenants in the leases so as to obtain the utmost money advantage, and that he meant in one instance, by the use of the covenants restricting the carrying on of trades, to throw a monopoly in the hands of a favourite baker, with the result of raising the price or lowering the quality of bread in the neighbourhood."

Here, again, we have an illustration of how the individual may suffer from the arbitrary use of the same power. Several years ago a correspondent wrote to a London newspaper as follows:—

"Two years ago I purchased a house on the Portman estate (eighteen years' lease) at £10 10s. per annum. I spent more than £300 to put it into tenantable repair, thinking that I should get a renewal at a fair ground rent. I applied and the agent came to inspect the premises, and a few days after sent me the terms as follows:—Lease for 34 years, ground rent to be £80 instead of £10; fine £1,000 renewal, to be paid from the day of application, or 5 per cent. interest on the £1,000 from that date, which would be principal and interest for eight years, £1,400; improvements to be done as stated in agreement, amounting to about £500, before a new lease is granted; all Viscount Portman's solicitor's fees to be paid by me. (For the simple drawing of this agreement I paid £15.) The last year of the 34 years' lease, the house to be re-decorated throughout; the property to be insured by me in the Portman Fire Office. Upon remonstrating at the exorbitant terms I received a letter from the agent that I could accept them or not, but in the event of my not accepting I should not have any further opportunity of applying." The remonstrant naturally asked: "What right can the landlord have to take my house? He has never spent a penny towards its improvement. Of course, the ground has increased in value, but that is through the tradespeople, and not through the landlord."[1]

---

[1] Letter of "Englishwoman" (Baker-street, London) in the London *Echo* of October, 1882.

Perhaps the worst evils of the leasehold system are found in that form which makes the duration of a lease depend upon that of several lives. The life system is nearly universal in Cornwall, or at any rate in the western part of that county. There land is leased to a person, not for a term of years, but for the duration of three lives, named in the lease. Directly these lives have expired, the land and the buildings raised upon it revert to the landlord, independently of the time which may have elapsed since the covenant was drawn up. The result of this obnoxious system of tenure—which has well been described as a "flesh-and-blood lottery"—is that property in great quantities and to great value, for which no equivalent has been given, often falls to a landlord owing to the early expiration of the lives. Thus the families and relatives of leaseholders are literally robbed of the fruits of the latters' providence, industry, energy, and enterprise. It is related that " on one estate in West Cornwall five farm leases on sets of lives 'fell in hand' within the space of ten years. This extraordinary occurrence was the result of an epidemic of typhoid fever, and here were seen the evils of the system in their most flagrant form. Not only was suffering entailed by a loss of life, but the grief of the survivors was aggravated by a loss of those means of subsistence which, under altered and more reasonable conditions, would have been still

E

at their command."[1] In another case a leaseholder in a Cornish village spent £260 in building a house on land held for three lives. All the lives expired in fifteen years, and the landlord became the absolute possessor of the building. An idea may be formed of the injustice which is suffered by leaseholders, and of the unearned increment which accrues to the landowners, owing to the existence of so inequitable a system of land tenure, when it is stated that no less than four-fifths of the house property in West Cornwall is believed to be held on life-leases. The injustice is intensified by the peculiar circumstances surrounding the leases. The population of West Cornwall is largely engaged in mining, and the duration of the miner's life is far below the average of the industrial life. Yet miners' lives inevitably condition the validity of a large part of the leases in existence. Moreover, the burden of proof of life does not rest now on the landowner, as it originally did, for it has been transferred to the leaseholder, who is allowed a limited time within which to furnish evidence when necessary. As the mining population of Cornwall is very migratory, this condition often proves a source of great hardship. Mr. H. Broadhurst, M.P., said at a leaseholders'

---

[1] See an instructive pamphlet called "The Bitter Cry of Cornish Leaseholders" for a full statement of the case. (Truro: Lake & Lake).

THE RENT SCREW. 51

meeting held at Camborne, in Cornwall, several years ago:—

"When in Devonport last night I was informed that there is at this moment in the Devonport Workhouse, living as a pauper, an old lady who ought to be in the possession of ample means to live in respectability and comfort, because sufficient property was left to her for that purpose, but she failed to produce evidence of the existence of a life on her property, the person having emigrated."

The Select Committee on Town Holdings reports to the same effect:—

"It is there a frequent custom for miners to insert in their leases their own lives, or those of others engaged in the same calling, and it is difficult or impossible to insure lives engaged in such a hazardous occupation. Cases of great hardship have been referred to where, from a rapid falling in of lives, families have been left unprovided for, and too often the death of the bread-winner may involve the loss of the home to the family. Another difficulty connected with insurance is, that the onus of proving the continuance of the life is usually cast by the lease on the tenant, and in the event of a person on whose life a lease is held leaving the country, the lessee may lose his holding through inability to prove the continuance of the life, and yet not have sufficient evidence of death to enable him to recover any insurance he may have effected."

For extremity of injustice, however, the following recital is unique. A contributor to Messrs. H. Broadhurst and R. T. Reid's handbook on "Leasehold Enfranchisement" writes from a Carmarthenshire village:—

"This is a large, straggling, mining village. All the houses and cottages have been built on ground leases by the occupiers on land belonging to one or the other of two proprietors. The leases granted are mostly for the term of ninety-nine years but the ground rents have been almost doubled in the last eight or nine years. I will call your attention to the following clause in all ground leases : ' That if any part of the said yearly rent shall be in arrear for twenty-eight days, the lessor may re-enter upon any part of the said premises in the name of the whole, and thereupon the said term of ninety-nine years shall absolutely determine.' A fortnight ago I heard of nine houses of which the ground landlords had entered into possession under this clause owing to the great fall in wages."

But one need not wish stronger condemnation upon abuses like this than is contained in a small work recently published by one who tells us that he " is himself a lessor or landlord, but he heartily deprecates the gross injustice of legalised landlordism, which gives the landlord the house that the tenant has built, and seizes everything in it to pay rent before other debts." This candid author says :—

"By the leasehold system the landlord is not content with taking the house that he did not build ; he also takes the goodwill of the trade attached to the house, and, on renewing a lease, extorts a heavy payment for allowing the tenant to continue to enjoy his own business which he has brought to the house, under the hard penalty of being turned out of the house altogether. The landlord's lawyers and agents are also allowed to make the burden heavier by adding new restrictive covenants to a new lease, with fees to be paid to them for the tenant asking permission to use the premises in any way that these restrictive covenants may prohibit. It is all cant to talk about freedom of contract where a tenant would be ruined if he did not submit to his landlord's terms."[1]

---

[1] "The Remedy for Landlordism," pages 32 and 33. Published anonymously.

CHAPTER V.

THE LAND MONOPOLY.

THE primary cause of the many evils—material, economic, social, moral—inflicted upon the community by the continued increase in the value of land and the appropriation of this increase by the owners of the soil, lies in the fact that land is a monopoly article. It is not, perhaps, generally recognised how powerful a body the land monopolists are. According to the Domesday Book of 1875 one quarter of the land of the United Kingdom was in that year held by 1,200 persons (the average being 16,200 acres each), a quarter by 6,200 persons (average 3,150 acres), a quarter by 50,770 persons (average 380 acres), and a quarter by 261,830 persons (average 70 acres). One half was held by 7,400 persons, and the other half by 312,500 persons. While 4,500 persons held half the area of England and Wales, 1,700 held nine-tenths of Scotland, a single owner having in his hands more than a million and a quarter acres.[1] The appended details

---

[1] The returns placed the number of landowners in the United Kingdom at 1,173,724, but the estimate was far too high, as it included hundreds of duplicates and thousands of leaseholders, and besides, 852,438 of the reputed owners held less than an acre of land, their average not being a quarter of an acre each. Recent

are instructive, but hardly gratifying. When the Domesday Book was compiled land was held as follows in the United Kingdom :—

England and Wales.
(Total area, without London, which the returns excludo, 37,243,859 acres.)

1 person owned	186,397 acres.		
12 persons ,,	1,038,883 ,,		
66 ,, ,,	1,917,076 ,,		
100 ,, ,,	3,917,641 ,,		
280 ,, ,,	5,425,764 (one-sixth of the enclosed land)		
523 ,, ,,	one-fifth of all England and Wales		
710 ,, ,,	one-fourth	,,	,,
450 ,, ,,	one-half	,,	,,
10,207 ,, ,,	two-thirds	,,	,,

Scotland.
(Total area 18,946,694 acres.)

1 person owned	1,326,000 acres		
12 persons ,,	4,339,722 ,,	(a quarter of Scotland)	
24 ,, ,,	a quarter of Scotland		
70 ,, ,,	a half	,,	
171 ,, ,,	,,	,,	
330 ,, ,,	two-thirds		
1,700 ,, ,,	nine-tenths		

Ireland.
(Total area 20,159,677 acres.)

1 person owned	170,119 acres			
12 persons ,,	1,297,888 ,,			
292 ,, ,,	6,458,100 ,,	or a third of the island		
744 ,, ,,	9,612,728 ,,	or half	,,	,,
1,942 ,, ,,	two-thirds of the island			

returns show that the number of separate holdings in France exceeds five and a half millions, and in Germany exceeds five and a quarter millions.

It is bad enough when the monopoly extends to rural land—to the soil that is cultivated, to the forest, and the moorland—but it is infinitely worse when a few persons, or perhaps one, can claim to possess the ground upon which a large community lives and has its being. There are many instances of this in the United Kingdom. In some cases a single individual practically holds the destinies of a town in his hands. The state of things even in London—heterogeneous as the city is in so many respects—is appalling, and a metropolitan journal only spoke too truly when it said not long ago :—

" Unquestionably legislation in some form will be necessary to reform a system under which nine-tenths of the inhabitants of the metropolis have no interest in their own houses, and the soil of London is rapidly passing into the hands of a few millionaires."[1]

Owing to the existence of a huge monopoly in land, and to the exaggerated estimate taken by landlords of their legal rights, society has been injured in a multitude of ways. Private enterprise has been harassed, projects of public utility have been thwarted, and their promoters exploited; in fine, society has been given to understand that the landlords do not exist for it, but it for the landlords. The history of railway enterprise is an apt illustration of the manner in which the interests of the community have invari-

---

[1] The *Observer* of September 23rd, 1888.

ably been made subservient to those of the landed class. The opposition of the owners of the soil has been a constant obstacle in the way of railway construction, and often the public convenience has permanently suffered by reason of the hostility of those through whose land projected railways would have passed. Then, too, the great cost of railways has generally been due to the opposition of the landowners, and the extortionate conditions on which they had agreed to part with the required land. Nobody now defends the monstrous imposition practised upon railway promoters in the past by many landlords. Not only did they demand exorbitant prices for their land, but they imposed an extra tribute of from 10 to 25 per cent. for compulsory purchase, not to speak of allowances required for "severance" (the division of an estate by the line) and other special circumstances, the money received being frequently double the real value, and even more. Mr. Brodrick says:—

"The landed interest of England is estimated to have received a sum exceeding the national revenue [1] from railway companies alone over and above the market value of the land thus sold."

And Professor Thorold Rogers recently wrote:—

"In the early days of railway legislation owners constantly got forty or fifty times as much as their property was worth, and, I regret to say, constantly in exchange for their votes in

---

[1] Mr. A. Arnold says £100,000,000.

Parliament. One of these persons, a man of rare integrity and honour, the late Lord Taunton, actually refunded to the Great Eastern Company £100,000, which he inferred had been paid to him for land in excess of its value."[1]

A natural consequence of expensive railway construction is that the public have to pay needlessly excessive rates for carriage. Thus the injury done by the landlords to the railway promoters in the first instance fell ultimately upon the entire community; and yet, while the landlords have done their best to prevent the construction of railways, and to make their construction as costly as possible, they have derived the principal benefit. Owing to the provision of railway facilities their land has often been given a vastly greater value. Agricultural land has become eligible for building purposes, and even as agricultural land its value has increased by the existence of improved means of communication and transport. Take the following extracts from land reports of recent date :—

"That the new direct line between Canterbury and Folkestone is materially assisting in the opening up of the country for residential purposes, there can be no doubt. Land companies already have an eye on it, having scented afar off the increasing demand for residences with from one to four or five acres of land within a few miles of Folkestone."

---

[1] Professor T. Rogers in an article, "Vested Interests," in the *Contemporary Review* for June, 1890

"The hundred of Wirral (Cheshire) is rapidly becoming the choice residential district of merchants and professional gentlemen carrying on business in Liverpool, to which there is excellent accommodation by rail through the Mersey Tunnel and the various ferries across the Mersey. Land is therefore in great demand for building purposes, as well as for the production of milk, butter, fruit, and garden produce for the Liverpool and Birkenhead markets. The new railroad to be made from North Wales to Liverpool across Wirral will so open up the various building districts that property of all kinds will be materially enhanced in value."[1]

Again, writing this year (1890) of Fort Worth, in Texas, two English visitors, Mr. S. Smith and Mr. B. S. Brigg, said :—

"A few years ago it had only a single railway ; its inhabitants were determined to make it a great railroad centre ; now there are eleven systems running into it, seven of which are great trunk lines. A glance at the map of Texas gives the impression that every company is striving to reach Fort Worth. The natural effect has been a wonderfully rapid development and a great increase in the value of property. One gentleman told us that thirteen years ago he bought a site for 300 dollars, and on it built a house, in which he has since resided, costing 1,000 dollars ; in February of this year he sold this property for 15,000 dollars. We heard 22,000 dollars offered for some plots that cost the present owner a short time ago 11,000 dollars."

Similarly, Mr. Henry George tells us that while the Transcontinental Railway which was to connect New York and San Francisco was in progress, the value of land in California grew enormously :—

---

[1] *Land Agents' Record* for January, 1890.

THE LAND MONOPOLY. 59

"Lots on the outskirts of San Francisco rose hundreds and thousands per cent., and farming land was taken up and held for high prices, in whichever direction an immigrant was likely to go." . . . "What thus went on in California went on in every progressive section of the Union. Everywhere that a railroad was built or projected, land was monopolised in anticipation, and the benefit of the improvement was discounted in increased land values."[1]

Where the land upon which a town is situated is monopolised by a single person, as is often the case, one of two results occurs: either enterprise is stifled (the condition of the community being stationary) or it is laid under heavy and unjust impositions. More to the purpose of this inquiry is the latter alternative, for we can here see how the primary effect of individual exertion and public progress is the unlimited enrichment of the owner of the soil. "One nobleman is known to have received three-quarters of a million sterling for the mere sites of docks constructed by the enterprise of others." Monopolists of this kind are able to dictate terms to a town's inhabitants—to say how they shall live, to lay down the conditions of their occupation, and to a great extent to determine the degree of their material prosperity. They may provide them with what dwellings they choose; they may favour an industry or stifle it; they may encourage trade, or drive it away. A correspondent of the *Land Agents' Record*, writing to that journal on January 18th, 1890, said of Folkestone :—

---
[1] "Progress and Poverty," Book V., chapter 1.

"The town labours under the disadvantage of being mostly held by one man, the lord of the manor, and the consequence is, that every building operation—nay, more, every proposed improvement of the Corporation's—is subject to the will and pleasure of his lordship, or of his agents. Appreciating his position to the full, the lord of the manor has but to await events, knowing that all who wish to build must apply to him for what amounts to *permission* to increase his already overflowing exchequer. He does not seek to open up his property for developing it by competition, but rather allows it to stand idle until a bidder comes along prepared to pay the exaggerated ground rent demanded. Mark: *none of the land is sold!* What is the result of all this? Why, that instead of there being fair villas, and other residences in their own grounds, dotted about, all are crowded together, with barely a piece of ground that can be dignified by the name of garden. . . The tendency of land and residential properties, a few miles out, is certainly to increase in value to a wonderful extent. Where, but a short time since, £3,000 was given for a small freehold residential estate, £6,000 is now confidently expected for it. A cottage and three acres formerly let at £30 a year cannot now be had for less than twice that amount. Land in the neighbourhood of Hythe, too, which some years since was bought for the proverbial 'song,' is now on sale and actually realises at the rate of £400 an acre."

The manner in which the land monopoly affects industry and commerce for ill in England is well dealt with by Mr. A. O'Connor, M.P., in the special report prepared by him as a member of the Royal Commission on the Depression in Trade and Industry (appointed in 1885):—

"What are the circumstances under which manufacturing industry is carried on in this country in respect of the use of land? With the falling in of leases so much higher a ground rent is charged that even with an increase of business there is less profit. Not only in London does the amount paid for the occupation of ground bear a higher proportion to the profits of trade than it formerly did, but in Birmingham too, where trade prices have been lowered, profit reduced, and wages are less, and where there are large numbers of persons vainly seeking employment, the price which has to be paid for the use of land has increased. The evidence on this point from Sheffield, again, was of the clearest; and it was shown that in Jarrow, which the shipbuilding industry may be said to have created, the landowners draw from the earnings of the industrial classes an immense income in consideration of the occupation of ground the improvement in the value of which is in no way attributable to them. And so of other places. As in the agricultural and mining districts, so in the industrial and manufacturing centres, the amounts which have to be paid for the use of land constitute a burden upon industry which is constantly becoming heavier, both absolutely and relatively." And he adds:—" It thus appears that over the entire country there is a cause at work—general, permanent, and far-reaching—affecting every branch of industry, in mine, and farm, and factory, the effects of which are traceable in the languishing condition of the agricultural, and the mining, and the manufacturing interests. That cause is the fact that under the existing land system the owners of the soil are able to obtain, and do exact, so large a proportion of the proceeds of the industry of the United Kingdom that the remainder is insufficient to secure adequate remuneration to the industrial 'classes, either in the shape of wages to operatives or reasonable profit to the organisers of labour, the employers, or capitalists."

Thus the land monopoly is not merely an abstract injustice; its injurious effects extend in all directions of social life. It is a wrong in itself, and it is a begetter of wrongs. The narrowness of this monopoly in civilised countries is the greatest cause of land speculation, with its attendant evils, which it is now necessary to consider.

CHAPTER VI.

LAND SPECULATION.

SO certain is it that in a progressive society land will increase in value, that there is now-a-days always a speculative element in the value of land. Men buy land with the expectation that it will, like wine, improve by keeping, and when it changes hands in the market regard is had not only to present but to prospective worth. It was stated in evidence before the Committee on Town Holdings that speculation in ground rents is very common in London. "Ground rents," said one witness, "are particularly favourite investments for investors who are more careful about absolute security and *the increasing value of the property in the future* than they are about a higher rate of interest," and the same witness estimated the gross value of the ground rents sold at the London Auction Mart alone in the years 1884-85 at £900,000.

Speculation in land, as at present carried on, may justly be regarded as one of the greatest evils associated with the institution of private property in the soil. Rightly described, it is nothing more or less than gambling over the probabilities and possibilities of social progress in one form or another. While the speculators benefit, the community as a whole suffers, and so long as the owners of land are entitled to appropriate the entire increase of value which accrues from the operation of social causes, this will continue to be the case. Illustrations demonstrate more readily than argument the evils to which speculation in land leads, but it must be self-evident that a practice whose effect is to create fictitious values and bloated rents cannot be a healthy one. It is not too much to say that but for the speculation which forces up the value of urban land to an unnatural height the grave evil of overcrowding, with its concomitant, the excessive renting of the working classes for the inferior accommodation afforded them, would never be heard of in our large towns.

It is a fact worthy of the thought of political students that this practice of speculating in land, in the hope of profiting by the progress of society—opposed though it is to the interests of the community—is nowhere more common than in democratic America. Dr. A. R. Wallace writes:—

"Land speculation, which we think is bad enough with us, is but a trifle here compared with what it is in America. In America land speculation is everywhere excessive. It is the great mode of making money, and it exists more or less all over the country wherever land is for sale and is not monopolised by great capitalists. Men buy land on speculation for the purpose of selling it again quickly."[1]

And the author of " Progress and Poverty " tells us :

" The man who sets out from the Eastern seaboard in search of the margin of cultivation, where he may obtain land without paying rent, must, like the man who swam the river to get a drink, pass for long distances through half-tilled farms, and traverse vast areas of virgin soil, before he reaches the point where land can be had free of rent, *i.e.*, by homestead entry or pre-emption. He (and with him the margin of cultivation) is forced so much farther than he otherwise need have gone, by the speculation which is holding those unused lands in expectation of increased value in the future."[2]

It is a common thing in America for people to speculate in land far West, where the trail of civilisation is still faint, yet where in time busy communities will no doubt plant themselves. This land is purchased in the certain expectation that it will increase in value as civilisation presses onward across the prairie. A man who invests to even a moderate extent feels sure that the augmentation of value will in time provide

---

[1] " Land Lessons from America." Again, the same writer says :—"An enormous proportion of the well-to-do people of the country either have made money by land speculation or hope to do so. . . The result of these speculations is that in the cities—in the suburbs of the cities, in the places where working-men live, we find the land cut up into still smaller strips than in England, and the houses are built still more closely together. . . Here you have private property making land the subject of speculation, producing all the evil effects, such as crowded cities and bad tenement houses, that you have in our great cities at home."

Mr. Henry George's " Progress and Poverty," Book IV. chap. 4.

him with a satisfactory competency. He may never see his land, and may only know its approximate situation from the map, yet it is year by year increasing in value and accumulating for him a revenue which he never earned. Such a man, to use Mill's words, "grows richer in his sleep, without working, risking, or economising."

A characteristic example of American land speculation is related by Dr. A. R. Wallace, in a record of his travels in the States in 1887. He tells us :—

"I stayed some time in a growing city in Iowa, called Sioux City, which has a population of 20,000. They were having what is called a land boom—every city tries its best to have one—we should call it a land fever; and the consequence was that land which sold at £10 an acre three years ago was selling at £150 an acre. It was two miles from the city, and it was sold with the idea that the city would soon stretch out and reach it. In the residential suburbs the price obtained was £4,500 an acre, and in the centre of the city it was £40,000 an acre. In the town of Salina, in Kansas, with a still smaller population of only 8,000, which was first settled by Colonel Phillips thirty years ago, land in the suburbs is now selling at £4,500 an acre, and in the centre of the town at £30,000 an acre. Here also they had a boom, and land had doubled in value in a few months."

Take also the following passage from a description of Texas published this year (1890) by two English visitors, Mr. S. Smith and Mr. B. S. Brigg, of Keighley :—

"In America the ownership of land is more widely diffused than with us. Almost every man you meet either is, or has been, or hopes to be, the possessor of 'real estate,' and he is generally wishful to own as much as he can possibly find means to buy. A wealthy and very shrewd gentleman in Chicago said to us:

'I keep myself poor by buying land, because I know that it is the way to make my children rich.' Another prominent man in Texas smilingly said: 'It is true I own thousands of acres of land, but I am often in want of a few dollars of ready money.'"

An extract from the report of a British Consul for 1887 will give an idea of the extent to which speculation is a factor in the growth of land-values in the United States. Dealing with the price of land in Los Angeles in that year, Consul Donohoe wrote :—

"The price of real estate has advanced steadily for the past four years, and in this city has reached such a figure that the prospect of a further rise can only be predicated on the assumption that within four years the population will have reached 250,000, which I think by no means improbable. The extraordinary demand for landed property is best illustrated by the fact that in this city alone there are nearly 2,000 persons paying licence as land agents. £8,000 was recently paid for a lot 20 by 100 feet, or at the rate of £400 a front foot; £600 per front foot was offered and refused for another lot in the centre of the city. At this rate an acre divided into lots 100 feet deep would be worth over £260,000. Upwards of 100 towns and settlements have been laid out within the past year in this district, and I am informed that there are 40 new cities on the line of the Atlantic and Pacific Railroad between Los Angeles and San Bernardino, a distance of 60 miles. At the first sales of lots in many of these new cities, in May and June last, many persons remained standing in line in front of the places of sale for more than 24 hours for the privilege of buying a lot. It has been stated, half seriously, that one can walk on 'city' lots from Ontario to Los Angeles, a distance of 40 miles. Several of these new-born cities are being built up very rapidly, and are increasing marvellously in population; many of them, however, are destined to revert to farming lands. The frantic speculation in lots in almost all the new cities has entirely ceased, and the 'boom' has to some extent abated throughout the whole district."

LAND SPECULATION. 67

A very different tale was told when the land "boom" was over. In a report, which well presents the reverse side of the picture of profitable speculation, Vice-Consul Mortimer wrote from Los Angeles respecting the gambling mania:—

"The area of the city of Los Angeles (40 square miles) was not sufficiently extensive for the speculators in city lots. Suburbs were laid out on every side, and upwards of a hundred 'cities' were projected within forty miles of this city. Many of these 'cities' have no inhabitants as yet, and never will have any. It is no exaggeration to say that city lots (50 by 150 feet) were surveyed and staked out in the county of Los Angeles sufficient for a population of several millions. In the period of the 'boom' lands were sold and resold at intervals of a few weeks, the price being considerably advanced on every sale. The small profits from the cultivation of the soil were despised, and many fine orange orchards and vineyards were neglected, the owners having purchased with a view only to reselling at a higher figure. Many of the new 'boom' cities have reverted to farming lands, and in others, where some improvements were made, and so many lots were sold that they could not be converted into farms, the value of the sub-divisions is merely nominal. I am informed that lots in Monrovia, which were sold during the 'boom' at from £3,000 to £4,000, cannot now be sold for £100."

The experience of America is the experience of older countries. Wherever there is social and material progress the land speculator is found building his home, for he knows that he can there live and thrive. The history of Berlin after the war of 1870 is very instructive in this respect. The success of Germany led to a remarkable awakening in the political, municipal, and commercial life of the metropolis. Building

F 2

began to be carried on at once upon a large scale, and furious speculation in land set in. Writing in 1873, before the fever had reached its height, Dr. Engel, the eminent statistician, enumerated many estate and building companies which were then making enormous profits on speculation in land in the periphery of the city. One of these companies had bought land at £21 per square rood, and sold it directly afterwards for £51. Another had purchased at £13 10s. per square rood, and sold at £37 16s. Yet another bought at £213 per Prussian acre, and sold at once at £450. "Thus," he wrote, "hundreds of thousands of square roods of building ground in the neighbourhood of Berlin have been bought" (in the early days of Berlin's phenomenal development) "and sold again, yielding millions of thalers to the first happy purchasers. What labour has been done," he asked, "proportionate to such profits? What injury is not inflicted by such high middlemen's profits upon the future tenants of the houses which will be built upon ground thus made so expensive?"

A strange anomaly in the incidence of local taxation—one to which reference has already been made—encourages speculation in unoccupied land in and around towns. This is frequently withheld from use, to the public detriment, because its owners count on increasing value. It does not matter to them that the

---

[1] See *Verhandlungen der Eisenacher Versammlung* (Leipzig, 1873).

residential requirements of the population demand that the land shall be built upon. They hold it as a speculation, and as they are not called upon—in England, at least—to pay rates upon its market value, but only upon the income derived from it, the expectation of rising value allows them to treat it for the present as dead capital. In large towns this practice of keeping land, eligible and eventually intended for building purposes, out of the market, leads frequently to scarcity and costliness of dwellings. All classes of the population suffer, but it is well known that the working and poorer classes suffer most according to their means. Speaking of house rent, Professor Thorold Rogers says:—

"The cost is greatly increased by the power which the law confers on corporations and private proprietors to withhold land from the market at a minimum of cost. It will be clear that if the law encourages an artificial scarcity, it creates an unnatural dearness. By permitting corporations to hold land in towns, and by allowing private owners to settle land in towns, it gives such persons a power of exacting the highest terms possible for the use of their property, by keeping it out of the market till they can enforce their price. To use an American phrase, taken from the slang of speculators, the Russells and the Bentincks, the Cecils, the Portmans, the Grosvenors, and the rest, with the corporations, have had for a long period a ring or corner in the land market, and can force buyers to give famine prices.[1] Now what

[1] "There are large tracts of land allowed to be idle in the outskirts of rising towns, like our own Kensington Fields (London), that they may be sold at a vast advance in price when required for building purposes. Some of our greatest fortunes have been made in this way, and yet these lands escape taxation as long as they are unoccupied." (Mr. S. Smith, M.P.)

is an injury to the moderately wealthy is oppression on the poor. It is well known that vile and loathsome buildings, probably the property of some opulent landowner, yield from the misery of their inmates a far larger rent than the plots on which the most luxurious and convenient mansions are built. The law which levies rates on occupancy instead of on property makes the evil worse, for it puts the minimum inconvenience on the person who holds the strongest position."[1]

The same testimony comes from the United States.[2] There, too, the land in and around large towns is frequently kept out of use for speculative reasons. This land so lying waste may not always be needed for building purposes, yet it would be of great utility if devoted to productive uses. Thus Mr. Henry George says:

"Within a few miles of San Francisco is unused land enough to give employment to every man who wants it. . . What is it, then, that prevents labour from employing itself on this land? Simply that it has been monopolised and is held at speculative prices, based, not upon present value, but upon the added value that will come with the future growth of population."[3]

---

[1] "Six Centuries of Work and Wages," pages 425 and 426.
[2] Speaking for America, Mr. Henry George says:—"If the land of superior quality as to location were always fully used before land of inferior quality were resorted to, no vacant lots would be left as a city extended, nor would we find miserable shanties in the midst of costly buildings. These lots, some of them extremely valuable, are withheld from use, or from the full use to which they might be put, because their owners, not being able or not wishing to improve them, prefer, in the expectation of the advance of land values, to hold them for a higher rate than could now be obtained from those willing to improve them." ("Progress and Poverty," Book IV., chap. 4.)
[3] Ibid, Book V., chap. 1.

' In any case the withholding of useful land from employment beneficial to the community, in the interest of private speculation, is a social wrong. The wrong is all the greater because, while suffering the injury and inconvenience caused by the landowners' cupidity, the communities thus denied the use of unemployed land on any save extortionate and impossible terms are often increasing the value of that land year by year and month by month. This the owners know; hence their reluctance to sell at a fair market value. It is a demand of pure justice that unoccupied land shall be taxed upon its selling value. This would drive into the market a great amount of urban land of whose use the local populations have great need. The owners would no longer be able to disregard social interests with impunity, for taxes and loss of interest would between them eat up the value of the land which they allowed to stand waste rather than dispose of it at a reasonable price. Moreover, with the introduction of such a reform the incidence of local taxation would be thrown over a wider area, and would therefore fall more lightly upon the individual members of a community.

Mr. John Morley stated before the Eighty Club on November 19th, 1889, that "in Kensington there is land vacant to the value of £1,700,000, practically not rated at all, while certain fields, with a selling value of

£400,000 are rated at £62 towards the relief of the rates."

This anomaly did not escape the notice of the Commission on the Housing of the Working Classes, whose report proposes that vacant land shall be fairly rated :—

"At present, land available for building in the neighbourhood of our populous centres, though its capital value is very great, is probably producing a small yearly return until it is let for building. The owners of this land are rated, not in relation to the real value, but to the actual annual income. They can thus afford to keep their land out of the market, and to part with only small quantities, so as to raise the price beyond the natural monopoly price which the land would command by its advantages of position. Meantime, the general expenditure of the town on improvements is increasing the value of their property. If this land were rated at, say, 4 per cent. on its selling value, the owners would have a more direct incentive to part with it to those who are desirous of building, and a twofold advantage would result to the community. First, all the valuable property would contribute to the rates, and thus the burden on the occupiers would be diminished by the increase in the rateable property. Secondly, the owners of the building land would be forced to offer their land for sale, and thus their competition with one another would bring down the price of building land, and so diminish the tax in the shape of ground rent or price paid for land which is now levied on urban enterprise by the adjacent landowners—a tax, be it remembered, which is no recompense for any industry or expenditure on their part, but is the natural result of the industry and activity of the townspeople themselves."

Not only does speculation lead to a false and variable equation as between land and other commodities, and to the exploitation of legitimate purchasers, as well as of the users of the land or the buildings erected upon it, but it produces unhealthy conditions of commercial and industrial life, and inflicts deadly injury upon the great interests of labour. This is strikingly proved by the experience of the United States, where, as already shown, land speculation is carried on upon an enormous scale. Mr. Henry George writes :—

"That land speculation is the true cause of individual depression is, in the United States, clearly evident. In each period of industrial activity land values have steadily risen culminating in speculation which carried them up in great jumps. This has been invariably followed by a partial cessation of production and its correlative, a cessation of effective demand (dull trade), generally accompanied by a commercial crash; and then has succeeded a period of comparative stagnation, during which the equilibrium has been again slowly established, and the same round has been run again. This relation is observable throughout the civilised world. Periods of industrial activity always culminate in a speculative advance of land values, followed by symptoms of checked population, generally shown at first by cessation of demand from the newer countries, where the advance in land values has been greatest." [1]

Or, to take testimony of quite recent date, the more convincing because disinterested and without tendency. A British consular report from Los Angeles and Wilmington for 1888 says :—

"For the past five years I have annually chronicled a remarkable growth in population, wealth, and industries in this district. The prosperity of the past has at last received a check, the extent

---

[1] "Progress and Poverty," Book V., chapter 1.

of which it is as yet difficult to determine. *Over-speculation in real estate* has produced its inevitable results. The cessation of speculation in real estate throughout this district has reacted on every branch of business, a large number of tradesmen have had to close their establishments in this city, and there are now hundreds of houses and shops to let where formerly exorbitant rents were readily paid."

The same report says :—

"In the past year wages have been reduced from 40 to 50 per cent., and thousands of good workmen are now out of employment."

Another instructive illustration of the ebb and flow of "prosperity" caused by speculation is furnished by the recent history of Johannisburg, in South Africa. On January 18th, 1890, an English land newspaper contained the following :—

"Some remarkable figures have been brought out in the development of a scheme for the valuation of all the properties in Johannisburg, the wonderful gold-mining capital of South Africa. The scheme is in the hands of a firm of surveyors in the city, in conjunction with the city sanitary contractor. Of the extraordinary value of property in this part of the world some idea may be obtained from the fact that the valuation of one square and part of an adjacent street—known as Marshall's Square and Commissioner Street—amounts to £2,000,000. At the same rate, it is believed, the value of the whole of the property in the town will work out to not less than £25,000,000. The Sanitary Board have power to levy rates not exceeding twopence in the pound, which is sufficient to produce a yearly income of over £200,000. This is a splendid revenue for a city of less than ten years' standing. Values, of course, must be taken into account in dealing with these figures. A pound sterling in Johannisburg is very different from a pound sterling in London."

So much for the bright side of the picture. Five months later (June) the English newspapers published " A Warning from Johannisburg " in these words :—

"The Rev. R. F. Appelbe, Wesleyan minister, writing from Johannisburg, warns intending emigrant miners from Cornwall and the North of England from going there just now. Consequent upon great stagnation in trade, many of the gold mines are stopping and many miners are out of work. For many months past typhoid fever has been raging in the locality, and the hospitals are full of fever patients."

A later report runs in a still more gloomy strain :—

" The collapse which we have all along expected in connection with the Traansvaal would seem to be near enough at hand. The extraordinary rise of Johannisburg has been followed by a descent into the very depths of depression. Men who were worth, in realisable scrip, from £10,000 to £100,000 a short while back are said to be practically penniless to-day. The prudent workman who had saved a small hoard shares the same fate as the reckless gambler. Youths who, having been office boys or barbers' assistants, suddenly made an ostentatious parade of their newly-found wealth, are engulfed in the flood of ruin which has swept over the Randt." [1]

And here it will be convenient to refer to the plea often advanced that speculation in land is legitimate, and that there is no difference between making profits from the sale of land and making profits from the sale of ordinary commodities. Those who hold this view forget or ignore the fact that land differs from every product of man's hands in that, besides being a necessity of existence—the maintainer of life, it is a

---

[1] The *Colonies and India* for September, 1890.

monopoly article. God made the earth as big as it is, and man cannot make it any bigger. There is so much land in the world, and no one, not even a Rothschild or a Vanderbilt, can add an inch to it. Hats, boots, and coats—manufactured goods in general—can be multiplied indefinitely. The supply is only regulated by the demand, and almost invariably the cost decreases as the demand is augmented. With the land it is otherwise: the absolute supply cannot be increased, and the cost grows with the growth of the demand. Moreover, in paying for the goods offered by the manufacturer, we pay largely for labour; but no amount of labour can produce land. It existed before man existed, and is not produced. Landed property is the one commodity of exchange in respect of which civilised society refuses to recognise absolute rights.

It may be granted at once, however, that it is impossible to artificially prevent the value of land from increasing. It would be absurd to try to check the operation of social forces which act from necessity. If there were no private ownership of land, but the State were the custodian and grand lessor, the value of that commodity would inevitably tend to increase, owing to a multiplicity of causes which act independently of private and collective possession of the soil. Yet while it may not be possible artificially to prevent value-growth, it is possible and expedient to check *artificial* value-growth. Were the unearned increment secured wholly or even in part to society, there would be less inducement to speculation in land, and the increase in its value would be dependent upon healthier and socially more desirable causes. Men do not speculate commercially for amusement or the mere love of excitement, but for money, and if there were no prospect—or little prospect—of contingent gain, the great inducement to land speculation would be taken away.

At the idea of resistance to speculation the individualist will raise his hands in alarm and remonstrance. But these pages are written on the assumption that the interests of speculators cannot claim any partial consideration in the adjustment of the important problem under discussion—or, indeed, of any problem affecting the well-being of society. Those who hold the views here expressed would not dream of prohibiting speculation in land; all they say is, that society is not called upon to sacrifice its interests to the speculators, or to offer to the latter any facilities for doing it mischief. It cannot surely be considered a social advantage that a small class of men should be able, owing to their possession of a monopoly in land, to force up its value to fictitious and fabulous heights; nor can it be regarded as desirable that the value of land should be increased in order to allow of speculators enriching themselves. The result is to create extortionate rents, which, so far as trade and industry are concerned, make production dearer, and thus injure the consumer, and, so far as concerns dwellings, compel the householder to disburse an excessive proportion of his income in the mere sheltering of himself and his family within stone walls. Apart from the gains which fall to the intermediary speculator who does not buy land to keep, but to sell, the owners of the soil pocket the public tribute paid in the form of increasing rents. For their part, the house occupiers suffer in two ways by the growing value of land: they must pay more for the dwellings they live in, and more for the articles they use and consume. It cannot be to the interest of society that the rents of town dwellings should average, say, £20 instead of £15, and should increase five or even two per cent. every year. If such an increase fell to the whole community, the evil would not be so great, for those who paid it would in one way or another reap the benefit; but, as matters are, it all goes into the landlords' purse.

CHAPTER VII.

OVERCROWDING IN LARGE TOWNS.

FEW social problems have of late years occasioned so much anxiety, alike to philanthropists, reformers, and Governments, as that which is offered by the condition of the working classes in our large towns. Whereever we find a great aggregation of population, combined with conspicuous commercial activity and material wealth—and these conditions are generally seen to be correlative—there may also be expected overcrowding, with the dependent evils of more or less unsuitable, if not uninhabitable, industrial dwellings and excessive rents.[1] These phenomena are common to both the

---

[1] The evil of overcrowding long ago attracted the attention of foreigners visiting our shores. The Spanish author of a series of "Letters from England," published in 1807, wrote :—" The dwellings of the labouring manufacturers are in narrow streets and lanes, blocked up from light and air, not, as in our country, to exclude an insupportable sun, but crowded together because every inch of land is of such value that room for light and air cannot be afforded them. Here in Manchester a great proportion of the poor lodge in cellars, damp and dark, where every kind of filth is suffered to accumulate, because no exertions of domestic care can ever make such homes decent. These places are so many hotbeds of infection, and the poor in large towns are rarely or never with-

Eastern and Western hemispheres, and the problem which they present is one of the most difficult, while momentous, which modern society has been called upon to solve.

Many causes contribute to bring about the overcrowding incidental to all large towns, yet it is safe to say that each of these causes is primarily attributable to the high value which has been acquired by the land upon which such towns are situated. The formation of this high value having already been explained, we have now to consider one of the most serious of its results.

Undoubtedly the utter chaos which prevails in the provision made in large towns for the housing of the working and poorer classes is to some extent due to the absence of any feeling of personal relationship between owner and occupier such as is found on the land and even in small urban communities. This is what the Royal Commission on the Housing of the Working Classes had in mind when it reported :—

"When the causes of the present condition of the homes of the working classes are examined, it will be seen how the property on many estates has passed for long periods out of the

---

out an infectious fever among them, a plague of their own, which leaves the habitations of the rich, like a Goschen of cleanliness and comfort, unvisited." ("Letters from England," by Don Manuel Alvarez Espriella. London, 1807. Vol. II., p. 146.)

effective control of its nominal owners, with the consequence of utter disregard for the condition in which it is kept."

In large towns the housing of the people is made more or less a matter of speculation. House property is not built and let for the purpose of securing a legitimate commercial rate of interest, but of extracting from the tenants the highest rents which scarcity of dwellings, advantage of position, and individual helplessness make possible.[1] The result is often to bring about a condition of internecine war, such as may be found at Berlin, between landlords and tenants, a relationship characterised by absolute extortion on the one hand and suspicion and ill-will on the other.[2]

---

[1] When Miss Octavia Hill—the philanthropic lady who has done so much to improve the housing of the working classes in London by purchasing old property and improving it into a habitable condition—was examined before the Royal Commission of 1884, the following question was put to her by Mr. J. Collings, M.P.: "As fast as your (leasehold) houses fall in, the ground landlords will take your property, re-sell it at a higher price, necessitating higher rents, and consequently the whole operation resolves itself into increased value in the hands of the ground landlords?" The answer was: "Yes."

[2] In few places are the relationships between landlords and tenants worse than in the German capital, as all acquainted with that city will testify. Take the following extracts from a form of lease common in Berlin (published in Dr. Engel's paper on "Overcrowding" in the *Verhandlungen der Eisenacher Versammlung* (p. 177, *note;* Leipzig, 1873): "The furniture which the lessee brings into the dwelling shall not have been acquired from a furniture dealer on the monthly instalment system, nor shall the ownership of the same be prejudiced by the rights of a third party, but it shall be his unqualified property, as well as all objects pledged to the lessor for the duration of this contract for the proper payment of the rent. Without the sanction of the lessor the lessee shall not remove a piece of furniture before

The leasehold system is responsible for much of the wrong suffered by the working classes in this respect. As house property built upon the leasehold principle reverts in time to the owner of the soil, it is to the interest of the builder to give to his houses just such a degree of durability that they will stand during the period of the lease. Speculative builders are not found willing to spend money to benefit the landlords. They will not expend more upon the houses they erect than is absolutely necessary in their own interest. Thus the leasehold system conduces to wholesale jerry-building. It is the object of the builder to make as much profit as he can out of his bargain with the landowner, and in order that he may do this the tenant

---

the rent fixed in this contract has been fully paid. Should this contract, including the house regulations, not be fulfilled in all particulars by the lessee, his household, servants, &c., the lessor is entitled to sue not only for the carrying out of the lease, but also for ejectment, and to require immediate removal without notice; the lessee is, however, bound to pay before leaving the full rent for the duration of the contract." Commenting upon these exactions, a leading Berlin newspaper observed :—"In all seriousness, the lessee dare not, without the landlord's permission, sell an old coat to a second-hand clothes dealer, or give an old pair of trousers to a poor man. The contract is like a rope which the landlord lays round the tenant's neck, so that he may strangle him at any time; and yet the landlords wonder that the bitterness against them daily increases."

In Dr. Engel's paper, above referred to, it was stated that at the Michaelmas term of the year 1872 "more than 200,000 persons were compelled by the ruthless rent-screw to leave their dwellings (in Berlin); scarcely a house escaping the effects of this unexampled migration of inhabitants. In not a few houses the change was, in fact, from roof to cellar." These statistics are nearly twenty years old, but the same state of things prevails at the present day.

must suffer. The evidence brought before the Select Committee on Town Holdings contains many condemnations of the leasehold system, and especially short leases. An Oxford witness said the builders of property held on short leases " Did not build substantially ; they were unwilling to build substantially. It is within my own knowledge that in the earlier days, before we were able to grant more than forty years' leases, the buildings were built so as not very much to exceed the forty years' term." Similarly, a Truro witness said, speaking for Cornwall: " Buildings put up on leaseholds in the country are to a great extent put up to last only for the term for which they are built, or as near as the lease can hit it, and are of the cheapest construction."

Again, a report prepared for the Corporation of Bury in 1888, on the Earl of Derby's cottage property in that town, says:—

" The worst class of property we have in the town is certainly that at present in Lord Derby's hands, and that built upon his land ; and from a residence of sixteen years in the town, the latter half of which I have been engaged as sanitary inspector for the Corporation, I have not the slightest hesitation in saying that I consider the present system of leasing land for building purposes is most pernicious in its effects on the sanitary state of the town. I have experienced the greatest difficulty in getting owners of property to carry out needed improvements on leaseholds, when they know that all they do goes to the benefit of the landowner. I have been repeatedly told by such property owners, even when there have been eight or ten years of their leases unexpired, that they will not make the necessary alterations and reconstructions to put their property in a good sanitary state unless they are compelled, as they would only be adding to what they consider a glaring injustice."

But an even worse evil than leasehold building is purely speculative building, whether leasehold or not. Here the interests of the tenants meet with less consideration still. It matters not to the speculator how unsubstantially his houses are built, so long as he can sell them at a profit and proceed to build others. The doors may be frail, the windows shaky, the stairs insecure, and the floors rotten and creaky; but these defects are only of importance so far as they spoil the builder's bargain when the houses pass out of his hands, for the property was built, not to be lived in, but to be sold. Well might the Berlin Social-Democrats, meeting 5,000 to 6,000 strong, adopt a resolution declaring "The scarcity of dwellings and the increase of rents in large towns to be a consequence of the social conditions of the present day, which make it possible for the owners of the soil to exploit the working classes by means of ground rent, and so carry on house building, not to meet the needs of the people, but for the sake of dishonest speculation."[1]

---

[1] Occasionally we read of representative bodies sacrificing not merely public interests, but the interests of the poor, to speculators. Evidence given before the Royal Commission for the Housing of the Working Classes (1884) showed that the Metropolitan Board of

It is inevitable—and experience proves it—that the domiciliary needs of the working classes in large towns must be worse provided for as population increases, for, as we have seen, increasing population implies the enhanced value of land. In other words, as a town grows the population of low-rented (*i.e.* industrial) dwellings tends to decrease. The working classes are gradually elbowed out of the way, and left to find shelter where they can. Statistics for Berlin covering the years 1815-1872 show that while in the former year 58 per cent. of the houses let at rents not exceeding £4 10s., this category had fallen to less than 5 per cent. in 1872. While in 1815 only 11 per cent. of the dwellings bore a higher rent than £15, the percentage in 1872 was over 40. And yet the houses offered for small rents had become far worse in regard to number and size of rooms, favourable position, and sanitary conditions. The experience of Berlin will be found to be that of all progressive cities and towns. This encroachment upon the dwellings which have sheltered the toilers is due, of course, to a variety of causes. The report of the Committee on the Housing of the Working Classes, for instance, enumerates five principal influences as opera-

---

Works used privately to sell land acquired by the demolition of decayed industrial dwellings—and which should have been used for the erection of new houses for the working classes—to speculators. A trustee of Peabody's Buildings complained that he had had to buy back a piece of land so sold at a premium of 40 per cent.

tive in this country: (1) the action of private owners who have sought to improve their properties; (2) the operation of the Artisans' Dwellings Acts; (3) the widening and improvement of public streets; (4) the erection of public buildings, as Board Schools; (5) railway extensions. While such private and public improvements as are here indicated are legitimate and desirable in themselves, we should not overlook the suffering which they often entail upon the working classes. And in this place it is impossible to leave unnoticed the harm and injustice too commonly done in large towns by the so-called "improvements" which consist in sweeping away wholesale old and decayed industrial dwellings without providing new habitations in their place. The effect of such "improvements" is simply to increase the overcrowding and its attendant rack-renting and misery. The report of the Commission on the Housing of the Working Classes refers to this question as follows:—

"The pulling down of buildings inhabited by the very poor, whether undertaken for philanthropic, sanitary, or commercial purposes, does cause overcrowding into the neighbouring slums, with the further consequence of keeping up the high rents." And again: —"The overcrowded state of Spitalfields is attributed in a great measure to such clearances; and the rise of rent, which has doubled in the Mint district, is largely owing to demolitions of the same kind."[1]

---

[1] "To quote an instance of the gross neglect of the interests of the poor by the State, take the working of the Artisans' Dwelling

Whatever the causes, however, which operate in diminishing the dwellings available in large towns for the toilers, none would be possible in the absence of a material prosperity which the labouring classes displaced do so much to create. Before the advance of wealth, labour must shrink into a corner.[1] *It* is the great factor in the production of that wealth, and it

---

Act. Space after space has been cleared under the provisions of this Act, thousands upon thousands of families have been rendered homeless by the demolition of whole acres of the slums where they hid their heads, and in scores of instances the work of improvement has stopped with the pulling down. . . . . So limited is now the accommodation for the class whose wage-earning power is of the smallest, that in the few quarters left open to them rents have gone up 100 per cent. in five years—a room which once let for 2s. a week is now 4s. Worse even than this, the limited accommodation has left the renters helpless victims of any extortion or neglect the landlords of these places may choose to practise. The tenants cannot now ask for repairs, for a decent water supply, or for the slightest boon in the way of improvement. They must put up with dirt, and filth, and putrefaction—with dripping walls and broken windows, with all the nameless abominations of an unsanitary hovel, because if they complain the landlord can turn them out at once, and find dozens of people eager to take their places who will be less fastidious." ("How the Poor Live," by G. R. Sims. London, 1883.)

See also a statement made by Earl Compton at a public meeting held in St. James's Hall, London, February 14th, 1889, on the industrial dwelling question :—"Another instance was that of the clearances for the building of the Law Courts. A thousand people had been cleared out, and no proper provision had been made for them. So it was in Chelsea; and he had been informed that Fulham was now suffering morally because people had been crowded into it out of Chelsea. Clearances and so-called improvement, which might be an improvement to the pocket of the ground landlords, but which were a detriment to thousands of inhabitants, must be prevented."

[1] "At the back of the 'richest street in Europe' (Regent Street, London) there lies a mass of poverty more depressing, in some respects, than that of the East End. In this part the three most

suffers because the wealth is produced. Every fresh stride which a town makes on the path to opulence leads to a rise in the value of land and a rise in rents. The working classes, whose ability to meet the demands of the house-owners does not meanwhile increase, are thus driven from a better class of dwellings to a worse, until they are found at last huddling in dilapidated rookeries unfit for human habitation, yet glad to secure mean shelter even there.

Let us first see what proportion of their incomes labouring families are compelled to disburse in the one item of house rent, and then the kind of accommodation which is often provided. It is unhappily a fact that there are in most large towns a great many working-men who, in order to pay the excessive rents demanded, have to rob those dependent upon them of proper food and clothing. How could it be otherwise when we find, in some cases, as much as half their earnings going to the landlord? The Inspector of Schools for the London School Board, Mr. M. Williams, furnished the Commission on the Housing of the Working Classes with valuable evidence on this subject. He showed that in the parishes of Clerkenwell, St. Luke's, St. Giles, Marylebone, and other poor quarters of London, 88 per cent. of the population pay more than

---

potent causes of poverty are: (1) low wages; (2) intermittent character of the work; (3) *high rents.*" (Rev. F. L. Donaldson in the *Pall Mall Gazette,* May 11th, 1890.)

one-fifth of their income in rent, 46 per cent. pay from one-fourth to one-half, 42 per cent. from one-fourth to one-fifth, and only 12 per cent. pay less than one-fifth. The average rent of one room, let as a separate tenement, is 3s. 10¾d.; of two-roomed tenements, 6s.; and of three-roomed tenements, 7s. 5¼d. In individual cases quoted by the Commission, 4s. a week was paid for a room 10 feet by 7 feet, 5s. a week for "a single room in a state of great decay," and as much as 6s. each for some rooms. To evidence like this was added the not very reassuring statement that "rents in the congested districts of London are getting gradually higher, and wages are not rising, and there is a prospect, therefore, of the disproportion between rent and wages growing still greater." A "Return of Expenditure by Working Men," published by the Labour Department of the Board of Trade, for 1889 gives some striking figures on this head. The following are a few samples, the working-men belonging to the better-paid class:—

| Total yearly income. | Rent, rates, & taxes. | Percentage. |
£ s. d.	£ s. d.	
52 0 0	14 19 0	28·75
150 0 0	35 10 0	23·66
28 12 0	6 14 5	23·50
50 0 0	11 14 0	23·40
44 16 0	10 6 5	23·04
80 0 0	16 8 0	21·13
55 0 0	11 3 0	20·27

What is true of England is equally true of other countries. Take the case of Berlin. Here house rents have risen continuously for many years. In 1815 the average rent of a house in Berlin was 39 thalers, or £5 17s. By the year 1830 the average rent was 85 thalers, or £12 15s. It was now that the industrial life of the city began to develop, and the result was a steady increase in rents. While in 1830 there were 51,794 dwellings, the number was 173,003 in 1872, and the average rent in the latter year was 171 thalers, or £25 13s. If we inquire how the working classes have been affected by this rise in rents, we find that whereas twenty years ago they paid 25 per cent. of their earnings to the landlord they now pay on an average over 30 per cent. Dr. Miquel, the new Prussian Minister of Finance, declared in the German Reichstag on January 20th, 1888 :—

"The working classes, especially those worst situated, pay in Berlin, Frankfurt, Cologne, Königsberg, &c., between 25 and 30 per cent.—and sometimes even more—of their total revenue in rent."

Again, as to France, in an article on "The Workmen of Paris, 1390-1890," Madame Darmesteter has shown that while the rent of the Parisian journeyman mason or fuller was £1 16s. a year in 1385, the rent of a Parisian tailor was £12 in 1885; otherwise expressed, while five hundred years ago rent formed one-twenty-fifth part of the journeyman's wages, it is now about a sixth.

So, too, Lord Compton said truly, in a recent article on " The Homes of the People ":—

" High rents are inflicting grievous harm on many who would otherwise have a better chance of fighting for a more prosperous existence. There can be no doubt that the poorer a man is the more, comparatively, he has to pay for his lodging. Everything tends to raise the workman's rent. Clearances and improvement schemes increase the competition for house room ; the sub-letting of tenement houses necessitates a profit to each one in the chain of leaseholders up to the ground landlord ; compulsion to live near their work raises the rent in a working-class quarter ; and if the man could live at a distance, perhaps his wife and daughters cannot. . . All these causes and many others not only produce overcrowding, but also exorbitant rents." [1]

And what is the character of the houses offered to the working classes in return for the large slice taken from their earnings? Of course, there are better and worse dwellings ; but in judging of laws and institutions from which abuses of the gravest kind are inseparable—whose inevitable effect is the production of dangerous social evils—we are justified in looking upon the darkest side. For damning evidence upon this subject it is not necessary to go further than the report of the Royal Commission on the Housing of the Working Classes. The Commission found that "the evils of overcrowding, especially in London, are still a public scandal [notwithstanding the " enormous improvement " effected during the past thirty years] and were becoming in certain localities more serious than

See *New Review* for June, 1889.

they ever were." The report gives the following London illustrations among others :—

"In Clerkenwell, at 15, St. Helena Place, a house was described containing six rooms, which were occupied at that time by six families, and as many as eight persons inhabited one room. At 1, Wilmington Place, there were 11 families in 11 rooms, seven persons occupying one room. At 30, Noble Street, five families of 26 persons in all were found inhabiting six rooms. A small house in Allen Street was occupied by 38 persons, seven of whom lived in one room. In Northampton Court there were 12 persons in a two-roomed house, eight of whom inhabited one room. In Northampton Street there was a case of nine persons in one room. At 5, Bolton Court, a family of 10 persons occupied two small rooms. At 36, Bowling Green Lane, there were six persons in an underground kitchen. At 7, New Court, there were 11 persons in two rooms, in which fowls also were kept. In Swan Alley, in an old, partly wooden, and decayed house, there were 17 persons inhabiting three rooms. In Tilney Court, St. Luke's, nine members of a family, five of them being grown up, inhabited one room, 10 feet by 8. In Lion Row there was a room 12 feet by 6, and only 7 feet high, in which seven persons slept. In Summers Court, Holborn, there were two families in a room 12 feet by 8. At 9, Portpool Lane, there were six persons in one small back room. At 1, Half Moon Court, in a three-roomed house, were found 19 persons, 8 adults and 11 children, and the witness, who has had much experience in the neighbourhood, said that he could hardly call that house overcrowded, as he knew of a case of 12 persons in one room in Robin Hood Yard, Holborn. In St. Pancras, at 10, Prospect Terrace, eight persons inhabited one room, 10 feet by 7 feet, and 8 feet high. At 79, Cromer Street, there was an underground back kitchen, 12 feet by 9, and 8 feet high, inhabited by seven persons. At 3, Derry Street, the first floor front room was 13 feet by 12, and 9 feet high, and was inhabited by a family of nine, who had only one bed. At 22, Wood Street, on the top floor, there was a room, 11 feet by 9, and 8 feet high, inhabited by a family of eight persons," adding that "evidence of the same kind was forthcoming from other parts of London," that overcrowding was likewise a great evil in provincial towns, both large and small, and that various other evils were everywhere found to accompany overcrowding, "sanitary and structural defects in the dwellings of the poor" being one. And yet,

"Notwithstanding the great change for the better, the evidence proves conclusively that there is much disease and misery still produced by bad drainage. The work of house-drainage is imperfectly done, frequently in consequence of there being little supervision on the part of the local authorities. There has been much building, moreover, on bad land covered with refuse heaps and decaying matter. The closet accommodation is most defective in spite of the extensive power confided to local authorities by the law in this respect. In Clerkenwell there are cases where there is not more than one closet for sixteen houses. In a street in Westminster, a witness stated that there was only one for all the houses in the street, fifty or sixty people inhabiting each house, and that it was open and used by all passers-by. In other parts of London a similar state of things was said to exist."

Again, quoting from the same report :—

"In York Place, Clerkenwell, the walls were described as so damp that the paper was hanging in shreds. In the neighbourhood of Tottenham Court Road the back rooms of certain houses are described as being dark because where the yard should be what is termed a cottage three storeys high was built within two yards of the back windows of the front house. Instances might be multiplied from other parts of London. At Bristol, houses stand back-to-back, with air and light blocked out. At Newcastle there are very tall houses in the old part of the city, built back-to-back, or with no proper yards, and at Doncaster there are a large number without any back ventilation. Even where the back-to-back system does not exist, houses are often constructed so that the inhabitants obtain as little light and ventilation as possible. . . In Bermondsey, houses were said to be rotten from age. In Southwark, houses were falling down from decay, and some of them had large cracks and holes in the walls large enough for a man to enter. In Liverpool, where extensive improvements have been effected, but where the death-rate is still unfortunately very high, houses were described to be in the last stage of dilapidation. The windows contained very little glass, and even the sashes had disappeared. Few of the roofs were rain-tight, and the walls were alive with vermin. In some cases the walls were crumbling away, exuding a green slime, and so rotten that a stick might be thrust through."

And further :

" In Draper's Place, St. Pancras, there was said to be a kitchen, 12 feet by 10, and only 6½ feet high, entirely underground, the ceiling being below the level of the street, and this was inhabited by nine persons. Evidence was given of the existence of inhabited underground cellars in the neighbourhood of Grosvenor Square which were damp, quite dark, and without any ventilation, and in which the inhabitants were never free from illness."

Eloquent testimony is also afforded by a " Special report on the sanitary condition of cottage property owned by Lord Derby in the borough of Bury," prepared for the Corporation of that town by the borough surveyor in 1888. Here is a single extract :—

"Dearden Fold is one of the oldest parts of the town ; the buildings are in a very bad state, the tenants often being snowed upon in bed in winter, as the majority of the bedrooms are open to the slates. There is not a single house with a supply of water laid on, their principal supply being from a pipe out of an adjoining farm yard, the water not fit for cooking purposes. A case of smallpox occurred in one of these houses about three weeks ago. Seven of these dwellings have been in Lord Derby's hands for thirty-five years, and the other four for over ten years, and in each case he threatened to pull them down as they came into his hands; but 'threatened lives last long.' The only thing that I can find of any moment that the landlord has done for the tenants is to raise their rents. The internal fittings in many of them, such as stairs, fireplaces, &c., I consider positively dangerous."

Summing up, this very significant report says that there are

"not fewer than 260 houses (in Bury) which are in an insanitary condition, by reason of being old and dilapidated, built in crowded or objectionable situations, or constructed in such a manner as to be injurious to the inhabitants thereof, and all of which are in Lord Derby's hands, the rents having been paid to him through his agent, for terms varying from one to thirty-five years. I have never known of any desire on their part to remedy the defects stated, or to render the houses more habitable or healthy; on the contrary, I have had to make frequent complaints in order to get alterations or repairs done which I considered absolutely necessary."

It is only right to say that the overcrowding which is so discreditable to many English towns—and particularly to London—afflicts other countries equally. A German newspaper, devoted to the interests of the working classes, said recently of Berlin :—

"There is overcrowding there. It is a consequence of the income of the people not keeping pace with the increase of rents. The result is that thousands of people in inferior positions, who formerly rented two and three rooms, are now compelled to be contented with two, but mostly with one. Thousands of industrial families living in the back houses of the overcrowded suburbs seek a way out of their difficulty by letting the single furnished room to two or three lodgers, while husband, wife, and children live in the kitchen. The travellers who scarcely know how to praise the brilliant Friedrichstadt and West of Berlin enough would do well to turn their gaze a little upon the *proletariat* quarters in the East and North. There even a Zola would probably learn and see much of which the boldest fancy would not dream."

That overcrowding prevails in Berlin is shown by the fact that of the 1,122,330 persons enumerated in the census of 1880 no fewer than 478,052 were living in tenements having but one room that could be heated, or an average of 3·75 inmates to a room; 302,322 in tenements of only two rooms that could be heated, or an average of 2·23 to a room; and 127,346 in tenements of three rooms capable of being heated, an average of 1·56 to a room; so that over three-quarters of the entire population lived in tenements of not more than three rooms that could be heated, and having on an average 2·51 inmates to a room. Leipzig was even worse off, the average numbers of persons per room being 3·84, 2·53, and 1·80 in the three categories named. The result of the excessive rents demanded is seen in the fact that of every 1,000 tenements rented in Berlin 350 were not held for a year, 196 were occupied from one to two years, 129 retained two or three years, 81 from three to four years, and only 244 over four years. In 1875, out of 166,043 small tenements 22,823 were said to have been over-crowded, and at the following census 22,890 were over-filled out of 198,640. All accounts agree that the condition of things in Berlin is now far worse than in 1880.

When we examine the physical and moral evils which follow in the train of overcrowding, it is found that they hardly allow of exaggeration. Exhaustion and enervation, noisome filth, festering disease, devouring epidemic, domestic disorder, discontent,[1] immorality, intemperance: these are a few of the effects of the human herding which goes on so extensively in all large towns. And could they be absent? Must not the effect follow the cause? How can the working man, and still less his family, hope to preserve health in the dismal, dark, and dirty room which has to go by the name of home, breathing a fetid atmosphere, inhaling poisonous odours from rotten floors and reeking walls, and surrounded day by day, week by week, and year by year by disease-breeding influences of all kinds? Such are his "conditions of life": it would be more correct to say conditions of death. Official statistics

---

[1] The newspapers for April 6th, 1890, reported that "a great demonstration" was held in Victoria Park, London, the previous day, "to enforce the need for fair rents and healthy homes. Resolutions were passed condemning the inaction of the Government and local authorities in not enforcing the sanitary laws, and urging tenants in the East End not to pay rents until their houses were made healthy and habitable."

represent the mortality of metropolitan districts in which overcrowding prevails as exceeding 44, 53, and even 70 per thousand. Where overcrowding does not kill, it very often keeps its victims lingering in physical torture, bereft of vigour, a prey to continual sickness, going through life without living. The report of the Commission on the Housing of the Working Classes says :—

"Among adults overcrowding causes a vast amount of suffering which could be calculated by no bills of mortality, however accurate. Even statistics of actual disease consequent on overcrowding would not convey the whole truth as to the loss to health caused by it to the labouring classes. Some years ago the Board of Health instituted inquiries in the low neighbourhoods to see what was the amount of labour lost in the year, not by illness, but by sheer exhaustion and inability to do work. It was found that upon the lowest average every workman or workwoman lost about 20 days in the year from simple exhaustion, and the wages thus lost would go towards paying an increased rent for a better house.[1] There can be little doubt that the same thing is going on now, perhaps even to a greater extent. That overcrowding lowers the general standard, that the people get depressed and weary, is the testimony of those who are daily witnesses of the lives of the poor. The general deterioration in the health of the people is a worse feature of overcrowding even than the encouragement by it of infectious disease. It has the effect of reducing their stamina, and thus producing consumption and diseases arising from general debility of the system whereby

---

[1] "Financially the working classes lose £3,000,000 a year in wages through illness, largely caused by unwholesome surroundings; and morally and socially the results of overcrowding are a danger and a disgrace." (The Bishop of Chester in a sermon preached in St. Paul's, June, 1890.)

life is shortened. Nothing stronger could be said in describing the effect of overcrowding than that it is even more destructive to general health than conducive to the spread of epidemic and contagious diseases. Unquestionably a large amount of the infection which ravages certain of the great cities is due to the close packing of the population. Typhus is particularly a disease which is associated with overcrowding, and when once an epidemic has broken out, its spread in overcrowded districts is almost inevitable. In Liverpool, nearly one-fifth of the squalid houses where the poor live in the closest quarters are reported as always infected, that is to say, the seat of infectious disease."

Nor do adults suffer only. Worse in many respects than the wrong suffered by the men and women who, from no fault of their own, are doomed to pass their lives in the overcrowded districts of large towns, is the injury inflicted upon their helpless and innocent offspring.

"There is a great deal of suffering," says the report just mentioned, "among little children in overcrowded districts that does not appear in the death-rate at all. In St. Luke's ophthalmia, locally known as the blight, among the young is very prevalent, and can be traced to the dark, ill-ventilated, crowded rooms in which they live; there are also found scrofula and congenital diseases very detrimental to the health of the children as they grow up."

The stern moralist may preach against the vices of the poor, but can he wonder that people struggling against such conditions do not all, or easily, keep in the path of rectitude? Man is the creature of his surroundings, and morality never yet throve where external influences, which contribute so greatly to the regulation of life and conduct, were totally bereft of a humanising tendency. The intemperance which is an unfortunate characteristic of overcrowded industrial communities is undoubtedly encouraged in a high degree by the conditions of daily life.[1]

But *cui bono?* Why expose the evils of overcrowding? What is the moral of the story? Simply this: that overcrowding is a consequence—and an inevitable consequence—of the ridiculously inordinate value to which land is forced in large towns. Were it not that the owners of the soil are able to appropriate the whole of the increment created by growth of popu-

---

[1] "Why," asked a German journal, a short time ago, "do so many thousands of honest working men fall victims in Berlin to the brandy-shop (*Schnapskneipe*) and tavern life (*Wirthshausleben*)? Simply because they have not homes worthy of men, and because they often only find there dirt and disorder."

See also the following passage in an article on "The Ethics of Urban Leaseholds," contributed by Mr. J. T. Emmett to the *British Quarterly Review* for April, 1879:—"Intoxication as a habit is a common consequence, a natural result, of under-sized, unwholesome rooms; and not the lower but the middle and the upper classes are the fabricators and maintainers of the leasehold system, which denies sufficient house accommodation to the poor. These classes are the real culprits in the case of metropolitan intemperance; and to them, much more than to the working-men themselves, the vice and misery of drunkenness are due. . . . The lower middle classes are sufferers in much the same way as the workmen; and, to escape the pressing evil, clerks and superior artisans and little tradesmen, who compose so large a part of the suburban population, leave their homes and lose their time and health and money at the billiard-room, the tavern, and the music-hall. This is the secret of the great expenditure on drink, a sum that in ten years would buy up every London ground-rent; and until this fact is understood no valid diminution of the drinking habits of the people can be hoped for."

lation, and by public and private enterprise, land could not have attained its present bloated value, for there would have been less inducement to speculation, and the landowners' monopoly would have been restricted.

The causes which have operated to increase the value of urban land in the past will operate—and that far more effectively—in the future, unless counteracted. Every year the land in and around our towns becomes more costly; in other words, the foundation is being laid for a progressive rise in rents.[1] Knowing the labourer's position, can we contemplate such a prospect with equanimity? Already the pressure upon the labouring population is too hard to bear; what will be the result if this pressure is increased? Thousands of pounds of industrial wages which should be spent on food and clothing have to-day to be paid to the landlords, because our laws recognise the right of the latter to the increased value which not they, but society, gives to their land. And still the tribute levied upon labour in the form of rent is increasing, though wages, if not decreasing, do not rise. Unless the growth of rents is checked, two alternatives are open to the working

[1] A statement, prepared by the London County Council, showing the increase in ratings in "back streets of various districts in the metropolis," representing the "normal increase of rateable value of houses at each quinquennial valuation," instances two properties whose value increased from 1875 to 1880, 6·44 and 7·44 per cent.; and two which increased from 1880 to 1885, 10·44 and 11·78 per cent. The latter increases are equal to 62 and 70 per cent. in one generation. If rents rise to this extent, will wages?

classes of our large towns: less food or worse dwellings —in either case a more miserable standard of life.

It is true that an effort has been made by the Shaftesbury, Torrens, and Cross Acts to deal with the evils of overcrowding and unhealthy dwellings, but the framers of these and similar measures have committed a fatal error in proceeding upon the assumption that the financial responsibility for the provision of healthy and cheap industrial dwellings belongs to the local communities, instead of to the owners of the soil.[1] Mr. Chamberlain demanded nothing unjust when he said that "the expense of making towns habitable for the toilers who dwell in them must be thrown on the land which their toil makes valuable, and that without any effort on the part of the owners."[2]

That we are, however, very far from attaining the legislative recognition of this fair claim is abundantly

---

[1] See Professor Thorold Rogers in "Six Centuries of Work and Wages" (edition 1886) :—" Where rent is the most important and the most increasing part of the cost of subsistence, as it is with the urban labourer, especially, the mischief is prodigious. The self-complacency with which some persons—owners of land to a great extent in London, for the temporary use of which the severest terms which the law allows and the market gives are extorted, to say nothing of taxes on renewal, equivalent to the appropriation of the tenant's goodwill—advocate the housing of the London poor at the cost of the London occupiers, and of course to the enormous benefit of those who hold this induced monopoly, and will be vendors under forced sales, would be absolutely amazing in any other country besides England." (P. 531.)
[2] *Fortnightly Review* for December, 1883.

clear from the indulgent treatment shown by the law, and more still the law's administrators, to the owners of dilapidated house property.[1] Even now such property is one of the best investments open in London to people without consciences.[2] The over-crowding and high rents prevalent in industrial quarters in the metropolis ensure the owners of tumble-down tenements high interest upon their capital, and the dearth of workmen's dwellings is, and must be, so pressing that there is no fear of these places being deserted. They will only be disused when condemned by the sanitary authorities, and the owner can always count upon liberal terms on being bought out.

Thus the public improvements made during recent years in Birmingham are estimated to have cost from £300,000 to £400,000 more than they should have

---

[1] "In the worst parts of London the ground rent is almost the whole of that for which rent is paid, and it is well known that when the Metropolitan Board of Works purchased the rookeries, they often paid for a filthy and dilapidated tenement the price of a mansion in a fashionable square." (Professor Thorold Rogers in his "Six Centuries of Work and Wages," edition 1886, p. 537.)

[2] "In the valuations of property condemned for human habitation, because totally unfit for it, it used to be the practice to take the rent actually paid by the miserable tenants, and of course to add to this the inevitable 10 per cent. In this way the price paid for getting rid of abominable dens, the removal of which was absolutely needed for the public health, cost the ratepayers more than well-built mansions in the best part of London did. It was a practice to speculate in these places, to cram them with destitute wretches, and make a profit out of what was even then an offence." (Professor T. Rogers in an article on "Vested Interests" in the *Contemporary Review*, June, 1890.)

done, solely because the dispossessed landlords have compelled the Corporation to purchase at fabulously high prices. "That being the amount," says the report of the Committee on the Housing of the Working Classes, "in excess over what the property [purchased and removed] would have fetched had it been disposed of in the ordinary way." The evidence given before this Commission by the London School Board's surveyor was that "the reason why so many unhealthy areas have remained untouched in the metropolis is the fear of excessive compensation;" and a Peabody trustee complained that "buildings in a bad state have been paid for enormously." Similarly, Mr. A. B. Forwood, speaking for Liverpool, said that "the money paid by the Corporation of that city to the people who owned bad houses was a very much larger sum than they were morally entitled to."

To sum up. The well-being of the working classes in particular—like the interests of society in general—require (1) that the unearned value of land—that value which is created by the operation of purely social causes—shall be diverted from its present channel in such a way that the community as a whole shall share in it; and also (2) that the incidence of local taxation shall be so modified that the owners of the land upon which towns are built shall bear a considerable share of the parochial expenditure which tends to maintain and increase the value of that land.

It is interesting to note that when there is no question of private sacrifice a Minister of the Crown can be found ready to advocate the recognition by the State of the doctrine that unearned increment belongs to society and to society should be returned. In its very instructive report, the Royal Commission appointed to inquire into the housing of the working classes proposed that legislative sanction should be given to the principle contended for, in the disposal by the State of the sites of several public prisons in London at less than their present market value, so that they might be utilised for the erection of industrial dwellings. In a memorandum to this report, Lord Salisbury expressly said that the Commission desired the State to sacrifice the increased value which has accrued through the growth of population and other social causes, adding :—

"It may be objected that such a sacrifice would constitute an eleemosynary expenditure. If the description were accurate the objection would be a serious one. . . But it seems to me that to call the proposed operation eleemosynary is straining the meaning of the word. It is the surrender of an increase which has become unexpectedly disposable—an increase which is caused by that very concentration of population which it is to be applied to remedy. But this excessive concentration on this particular area is in more than one respect the State's own work. If the size of London is excessive the excess is largely due to the circumstance that London is the residence of the Government. If vast masses of the population are forced to live near the centre of the town and find no room for their dwellings, it must be remembered that the State has largely contributed both to swell the population and to diminish the house-room. The number of persons who are in the public service as soldiers, policemen, postmen, and employés in the lower grades of the public offices, constitute a notable portion of the crowds who compete for house-room. The forcible destruction of dwellings authorised by Parliament during the last half century, for purposes of public ornament or utility, has largely contributed to diminish the aggregate of the house-room for which these crowds have to compete. A proposal to remedy overcrowding, for which the State is largely responsible, by utilising a gain on enhanced value of land which is due to density of population can hardly be called eleemosynary. It more closely resembles the provision of compensation than the offer of a gift."

In accordance with this recommendation, Lord Salisbury in 1885 introduced in the House of Lords a Bill, the third clause of which laid down that—

"It shall be lawful for the justices of the peace for the county of Middlesex, if the justices think fit so to do, to sell and convey those respective sites or any part or parts thereof to the Metropolitan Board of Works at such price, to be fixed by agreement or arbitration, as will enable the Board *without serious loss* to appropriate the sites or parts so conveyed for the purposes of the Labouring Classes Lodging Houses Acts, 1851 to 1867, as amended by this Act."

It is only fair to the Conservative Upper House to say that while it passed this heroic clause the House of Commons so altered it as to spoil it, and Liberals could be found ready to object to its supposed "Socialistic" tendency. To such an extent are enlightened English politicians held in bondage to phrases.

CHAPTER VIII.

END OR MEND?

IT is necessary now to consider more fully than hitherto the question, cannot society with right claim the increased value given to land by distinctly social causes? We have seen the various factors which tend to create what is generally known as "unearned increment." In one sense this term is very inaccurate. The increment is by no means unearned; what is meant, when the phrase is used, is that the landowner has not earned it. Society, however, has; and earned it honestly by heavy toil, by exertion of body and brain, by plodding industry, by bold enterprise, by culture and enlightenment, by progress in numbers, in wealth, and in morality. There is not a yard of land in the country—be it used for the growing of corn, the pasturing of cattle, or the habitations of men—whose value has not been enhanced by these social causes. It was the settlement of men with their various activities upon the land which originally gave it value, and the increase of population has been a constant and potent factor in value-growth since the primitive communities first established the institution of private property in the common soil. And yet, while society has for centuries been growing and labouring to increase the value of the land it required for its food, its industries, and its habitations, it has ever done so to its own detriment. While enriching the landlords it has impoverished itself.

This, indeed, is the greatest anomaly presented by the social increment problem. As a community develops and prospers, owing to its energy, enterprise, and enlightenment, it is all the time preparing a rod, armed with which the landlords will sooner or later turn upon it. A town's residents are punished for their industry and merited success by having to pay the landlords more and more money for the land they use. Did not tradesmen, by dint of perseverance and pluck, succeed and thrive, the demands made upon them would not increase; but simply because they reap in prosperity the reward of exertion, the landlords require growing tribute in the form of higher rents. And so it is in all departments of social life. In the eyes of the owners of the soil, human communities become, in fact, simply value-creators, rent-producers. The landlords reap where they have not sown, they gather where they have not strawed. Little of the value of that land which they lend and sell, at prices which are often so fabulous, has been created by them, yet they appropriate it all.

In the words of Mill :—

"The ordinary progress of a society which increases in wealth is at all times tending to augment the income of landlords ; to give them both a greater amount and a greater proportion of the wealth of the community, independently of any trouble or outlay incurred by themselves. They grow richer, as it were, in their sleep, without working, risking, or economising."[1]

Or, to use the words of a later political economist of high authority, Professor Thorold Rogers :—

"Every permanent improvement of the soil, every railway and road, every bettering of the general condition of society, every facility given for production, every stimulus supplied to consumption *raises rent*. The landowner sleeps, but thrives. He alone, among all the recipients in the distribution of products, owes everything to the labour of others, contributes nothing of his own. He inherits part of the fruits of present industry, and has appropriated the lion's share of accumulated intelligence."[2]

But because society has made such enormous sacrifice in the past, should it do so in the future ? Surely the question is a grave one. We have seen the results which have been produced by the abuse of the institution of private property in land, which allows the owner to monopolise the value which is created, not by him, but by society. Briefly summarised, those results are : fabulous land-values and rents in towns, with terrible overcrowding and degradation of the working classes in large centres of population ; the over-burdening of agriculture and the harassing of

---

[1] "Principles of Political Economy," Book V., chap. ii., section 5.
[2] "Political Economy," chap. xii.

industry, entailing dear production and high prices; unhealthy land speculation, deranging commerce and often inflicting ruin upon the labouring classes; with social and political evils of many kinds. To these results we have already arrived, and all thoughtful people will acknowledge their enormous gravity. Are we prepared to face the intensification of the dangers now existing? Unless the system is modified, no power on earth will prevent it from yielding the same evils—the same in character, yet unspeakably more serious in degree. Shall society, then, suffer in the future as in the past, or shall it determine that these things shall no longer be? Shall it

"Take arms against a sea of troubles,
And by opposing end them?"

And here I would make it clear that I do not deny the right of every landlord, of every capitalist, to due reward for his expenditure, whether of labour or of money. For the capital invested in land, for the skill and exertion employed in its improvement, it is right to expect proper recompense. But when allowance has been made for a fair return upon these, there is still in the increment constantly accruing to the value of land a *social* element which is often found far to exceed the just deserts of the owner's investment, industry, and ability. It is with this *social* value that we have to do, and to whom should it go—to the landlord who did not produce it, or to society which did? Surely justice, equity, expediency, and common-sense unite in saying that the *purpose* of social institutions, social life, and social activities is not to enrich the incomes of the landlords—whatever be the actual fact under present circumstances—but that social progress should, primarily and ultimately, conduce to social benefit.[1] It is evident that such a reform as is here advocated could not be retrospective. As law and custom have encouraged the landlords to keep all themselves hitherto, we should have to make a new beginning, to start with a clean page ; we should have to let bygones be bygones, and forgive the past even if we could not forget it.

All sorts of remedies and half-remedies—from land nationalisation to leasehold enfranchisement—are proposed by men who believe that the community is not justly treated by the property-owners. Among the latest proposals advanced for the better protection of urban occupiers against the exactions of landlords are fixity of tenure and compensation for improvements. In other words, it is asked that the occupier shall have a legislative guarantee that his own improvements, whether caused by expenditure of capital or commercial

---

[1] "The question of unearned increment will have to be faced before many years are over. It is unendurable that great increments which have not been earned by those to whom they accrue, but have been formed by the industry of the community, should be absorbed by those who have contributed nothing to that increase." (Mr. J. Morley in the House of Commons, May 6th, 1890.)

enterprise, shall not be employed by the landlord as a weapon of extortion, and that on removal he shall be recouped for such monetary sacrifice as has increased the value of the premises occupied. A demand like this is not unjust, and the Select Committee on Town Holdings has approved it, but it is clear that, even if we secured the individual against injustice on the part of the landlord, we should not exhaust society's claim against the owners of the soil. We have still to consider increased value due to growth of population, the development of trade and industry, the increase of national prosperity, and public improvements—causes which are distinctly social. Here the individual has no claim, but the community alone.¹ Those who hold this view cannot but recognise the utter inadequacy of measures like Urban Compensation for Improvement Bills, Leasehold Enfranchisement Bills,² and even

---

¹ See the report of the Select Committee on Town Holdings:—"The grievance that the increased value of the land through public improvements or the progress of the neighbourhood goes to the landowner is so closely connected with the question of the taxation of ground rents, upon which we are not prepared to report, that we defer the consideration of it for the present, and only remark, as regards the increase in value arising from the collective exertions of the community, usually referred to as the 'unearned increment,' that although there may be much to be said against this increase in value going to the lessor, who may have done nothing to earn it, yet no good reason appears to have been put forward why it should be given to the lessee, who may have done no more."

² The principle underlying Mr. Broadhurst's Leaseholder's Bill of 1885 is optional power of purchase by the leaseholder. "The leasehold tenure," to use Mr. Broadhurst's words, "should be so

Agricultural Holdings Acts. These measures would still exclude society at large from participation in the unearned increment or social value given to the land. The only merit they possess—and merit it certainly is—is that they would divert that increment, that value, from the few channels into the many.

In fact, the principle involved in these proposals only furnishes us with a foundation upon which to construct a thorough-going measure of reform. The English legislation which approaches nearest to the ideal to be striven after is that passed in the interests of the tenant-farmers of Ireland. The Irish Land Acts are based upon the principle that the cultivators, the rent-payers, should not be rented upon their own improvements; that their exertions and expenditure of capital should not be made a source of greater gain to the inactive owners of the soil. From time immemorial it had been the habit of most Irish landlords to permit or compel their tenants to increase the productiveness of their holdings only in order that they might demand more rent.[1] Often land was originally

---

altered that a lessee shall be enabled to expend money upon the land, with the certainty that where he has sown there also will he reap: in other words, that he can become the owner if he pleases."

[1] Mr. John Bright said in 1881, when speaking on the second reading of the Irish Land Bill of that year:—"If you complain that the Bill gives too much to the tenants and takes all that it does give from the landlords, I should make this answer: If at this moment all that the tenants have done were gone, and all that the landlords have done were left, . . . the land would be as

let in a totally sterile and uncultivated condition—" as in the beginning of the world," to use the emphatic phrase of a suppliant of one of the Irish Land Courts a year or two ago—and just as its productive capacity was developed the landlord increased the rent, taking care that the margin of profit, if any, left to the cultivator, was so small as to compel him to redoubled efforts.[1] Thus landlords who purchased undeveloped

---

bare of house and barn, fences and cultivation, as it was in prehistoric times. It would be as bare as an American prairie where the Indian now roams, and where the white man has never trod. . . . I believe, and I think I am within the mark, that nine-tenths—excluding the towns, of course—of all that is to be seen on the farm land of Ireland—the houses, barns, fences, and whatever you call cultivation, or freeing land from the wilderness—have been placed there by the labour of the tenantry of Ireland, and not at the expense of the landlord." This is hardly an overstatement of the testimony furnished by the various Land Commissions which have inquired into the wrongs of the Irish tenant-farmers.

[1] "Now the Irish question was this: that in a vast majority of small holdings, under £10 a year, comprising half the population of Ireland, and to a considerable extent in larger holdings, the landlord had contributed nothing but poor, rocky, and boggy soil, worth certainly on the average not half-a-crown an acre, and often not worth sixpence, of annual rent, while the tenant had built the houses, drained, fenced, and reclaimed the land, and made all the improvements which had created a property worth, say, 15s. or 20s. an acre. Was the law just which entitled the landlord to take the whole or the greater part of this 15s. or 20s., and to leave the other partners, who had created fully three-fourths of the value, nothing but a bare subsistence in a condition of poverty unmatched in any other civilised country." (Mr. S. Laing in the *Contemporary Review* for April, 1890; article, "Aristocracy or Democracy.")

It would be an easy task to adduce hundreds of instances illustrating the point under consideration. The following is taken because it is recent. The narrative is a report of an application made before a justice of the Land Judges' Court in Dublin in

estates for the proverbial old song were able in time to derive large revenues from them.[1] This state of things was changed by the Land Acts

December, 1886 :—" An application was made on behalf of Denis Cronan and ten other tenants of the lands of Nadallerbeg portion of the estate in this matter, for an abatement of 75 per cent. on the rents due. The lands are situate among the Nad mountains, near Banteer, in the county of Cork. The affidavit of the tenants set forth that the lands are poor mountain lands which were reclaimed by the tenants or their predecessors, and on which the landlords had not laid out one shilling for improvements. Until 1872 the lands were held by those tenants or their predecessors under lease. On the expiration of the lease in 1872, ejectments were brought, and under pressure of those, and upon the faith of promises then made in writing by the landlords to make roads to the holdings, and to build houses for some of the tenants, and supply slate and timbers to others, new lettings were made at rents more than four times the amount of the previous ones. The affidavit further states that these rents are excessive rack-rents, which the tenants are absolutely unable to pay. The landlords never since made the roads, nor built the houses, nor supplied the slate or timber which had been promised."

The following figures show some of the decisions of the court:—

	Rent payable up to 1872.				Rent fixed in 1873.		
	£	s.	d.		£	s.	d.
Denis Cronan ...	... 5	6	0	...	26	11	7
John Ahern ...	... 3	10	8	...	15	12	0
Mrs. Kiely ...	... 1	5	4	...	7	19	6
Sandy Driscoll	... 2	13	0	...	8	5	9
John Thohig ...	... 1	6	6	...	7	6	3
James Thohig ...	... 1	6	6	...	6	12	6½

(Related by Mr. J. J. Clancy in the *Contemporary Review* for July, 1889.)

[1] " In the notorious Falcarragh estate it has been stated in open court—and the figures have never been contradicted—that the ancestors of the present proprietor bought it originally for something like £500, that the landlords have never expended a shilling on improvements, and that the rental before the passing of the Land Act was £2,500 a year, and is still nominally from £1,500 to £2,000." (Mr. S. Laing in *Contemporary Review* for April, 1890 ; article, "Aristocracy or Democracy.")

of 1870, 1881, and 1887. Tenants in general now have fixity of tenure, fair rents, and compensation for improvements. They can no longer be rented upon their own improvements, and on quitting their holdings they are secured indemnification for the increased value they have given to them by the expenditure of labour and money.

What has been done for the individual agriculturist in Ireland, and to some extent in England, should be done for the community as a whole. Society should no longer be rack-rented upon *its* improvements—upon the higher value it gives to the land, whether it be agricultural or town or mineral land; that it should no more be compelled to pay to the landlords a penalty for its progress, for the privilege of prospering, in the form of increasing rent.

CHAPTER IX.

MINES AND MINERAL ROYALTIES.

SPECIAL reference to the subject of mines and mining royalties is necessary, as it furnishes us with a powerful argument in favour of the appropriation by society of the unearned increment. The land nationaliser says it is indefensible that the ownership of the soil should carry with it a monopoly of the mineral wealth concealed below the earth's surface. However strong it may be possible to make the position so taken up, I do not approach the question of mining rights from the standpoint of land nationalisation. All that can be claimed here is that in future the unearned increment accruing from mines shall go to society. Whatever injustice may have been done to society in the past, and whatever the injustice which may still for a time be suffered owing to the legal recognition, hitherto, of a landowner's claim to the minerals beneath the soil, it is impossible to enforce a retroactive measure of reform; all that we can do is properly to protect society's interests for the future. In other words, the *present value* of mines now opened should be secured to the recognised owners, but future increased value and also undiscovered mineral wealth should become a common possession, with the reservation that an adequate return should be made for the capital and labour expended in the creation of that increased value, and in the opening of new mines.

Society has a peculiarly strong claim to share—and that liberally—in the wealth yielded by mines, because the owners of the soil, who now practically monopolise it all, have had no part in creating the riches which fall into their laps, and because it is solely owing to social needs that the unproduced mineral wealth of the earth becomes a source of such enormous gain to the landlords. It is not due to the latter's exertion that coal, iron, and lead are valuable articles of merchandise, and the accidental occurrence of minerals beneath the soil which they till should not be allowed to secure to them absolute ownership. All the minerals controlled by the Dudley family would be of little value to them but for the existence of industries which require these minerals. The enormous wealth—extending to millions of pounds—accumulated by this family was not made in remote years, but comparatively recently, since the development of England's great industries.[1] Here is an instance of

---

[1] In the course of a notice of the death of the first Earl of Dudley

how society enriches the owners of land containing mineral wealth; it sets forth the principle clearly, though not so emphatically as might be :—

" There is a mountain valley in Wales which might have been worth, at the outside, £800 a year as a sheep farm. But coal and iron were found, works created, and a town of 10,000 inhabitants sprang up, and the landlord now gets a secure income of £8,000 a year. The extra value has been created by the outlay of capitalists, most of whom lost their money, and by the labour of the community who live on the soil." [1]

Thus, too, we find Mr. Henry George writing :—

" The coal and iron fields of Pennsylvania, that to-day are worth enormous sums, were fifty years ago valueless. What is the efficient cause of the difference ? Simply the difference in population. The coal and iron beds of Wyoming and Montana, which to-day are valueless, will in fifty years from now be worth millions on millions, simply because in the meantime population will have greatly increased." [2]

It is well known that the landowners generally secure their share in the proceeds of mining in the

---

the *Daily Telegraph* stated, May 9th, 1885 :—" In 1835 [he] succeeded, as Lord Ward, to one of the noblest fortunes in the United Kingdom, of which he has been in possession exactly 50 years. Assuming—and the estimate is a low one—that his income had averaged £100,000 per annum for half a century, it will be seen that at least five millions sterling must have passed through his hands. In the year when the coal famine was raging with great intensity it was currently reported that the late Lord Dudley was in receipt of an income, derived from his coal and iron mines in Staffordshire, which amounted to not much less than one million of pounds in that single twelvemonth."

[1] Mr. S. Laing in article "Aristocracy or Democracy," in the *Contemporary Review* for April, 1890.

[2] " Progress and Poverty," Book IV., chapter 2.

form of royalties, rents, and way-leaves. By levying these tributes they are able to obtain a maximum of gain with absolutely no risk, with no possibility of loss. It is of no consequence to them whether mining is remunerative to the capitalist, so long as a fixed royalty is paid to them upon every ton of minerals produced. Thus when profits and wages fall, owing to the low prices ruling, the landowner's proportionate share in the revenue of a mine actually increases. The gains of the real workers of the mine—the men who provide the money and the labour requisite to its development—may come and go, but the owner's royalty goes on for ever. The evidence laid before the Royal Commission on the Depression in Trade and Industry, whose final report was issued in December, 1886, showed that in the county of Durham there was then a reduced output of coal, and prices had declined; yet, "while the workmen obtain lower wages, and the employer little or no profit, the burden of royalties is greater." It was also "given in evidence that in the Barrow district the royalties have increased in spite of the decrease in the price of iron.

According to Sir I. L. Bell the royalties on a ton of pig iron from ironstone, coal, &c., amount to 3s. 6d. in the Cleveland district, 6s. in Scotland, and 6s. 3d. in Cumberland; while in Germany the amount would only be 6d., in France 8d., and in Belgium 1s. 3d. to

1s. 4d. It was stated before the Royal Commission on Depression in Trade that during the years 1872 to 1875 iron ore on the West Coast of England was leased on royalties as high as 10s. a ton. In Cornwall the mine dues vary from one-fifteenth to one-twenty-fourth of the produce. No wonder that enormous revenues should often be made by English and Scotch landowners out of the minerals which chance to be found in their estates. The fabulous gains of the Dudley family have been noticed, and similar cases might be named.

When, a few years ago, a deputation of Members of Parliament had an interview with the Home Secretary on the question of royalties, Mr. Mason, who spoke for the Lanarkshire miners, said that in that county "one man received no less than £114,000 per annum in mining rents and royalties, or as much for doing nothing as 1,800 miners would earn in 52 weeks." A Cornish representative also instanced the recent renewal of Dolcoath mine lease for 21 years, in consideration of which the landlord had demanded £25,000. As to Cleveland, official returns show that the ironstone output of that district during the years 1849 to 1886 (thirty-seven years) was 130,909,946 tons, on which no less than £3,000,000 was paid in royalties. Again, according to the Secretary of the Fife and Clackmannan Miners' Association the output of coal in Fife and Clackmannan in 1874 was 1,588,000 tons. This output, calculated at 9d. per ton,[1] gave the landlords about £59,000 in that year. The output continued to increase till 1884, when it reached 2,044,000 tons, increasing the revenue of the landlords to £91,000—a clear increase of £32,000 per year going into the pockets of the landlords, who meantime performed no new or more valuable service in return; and still the average wages of the miners in the two counties were in the latter year only 15s. a week.

As it is in the power of the landlords to impose whatever royalties they choose, the fortunes of the mining industry largely depend upon their caprice. Without risking a penny of capital himself, the owner of mineral land may be able to make or mar the adventurers who sink thousands of pounds in the opening up of his mines: whether they obtain a fair return upon their investments or are reduced to ruin depends—apart from the capabilities of the mine— upon the moderation of his demands.[2] The capitalists

---

[1] Coal royalties in England, Wales, and Scotland vary considerably. Thus—Yorkshire, 4d. to 9d. per ton; Lancashire, 6d. to 1s.; Durham and Northumberland, 4d. to 10d.; Staffordshire, Midlands, 6d. to 8d.; Wales, 6d. to 1s.; Scotland, 4½d. to 1s. 4d. On the whole rents, way-leaves and royalties are estimated to be equivalent to an average tax of 8d. per ton on all the coal produced.

[2] In an article on "The Discovery of Coal near Dover," published in the *Contemporary Review* for April, 1890, Professor Boyd Dawkins says :—"The discovery of these hidden coalfields is a question of national importance well worthy of the attention of

are helpless, and not only they, but the miners and associated workpeople whose employment and wages depend upon a mine's successful and profitable working.[1]

It may be said that while a landowner certainly has the power of abusing his privileged position to the injury of both capitalist and labourer, the power is only nominal and is never used; and, therefore, that the dangers just indicated are perfectly imaginary. Unfortunately, however, the contrary is the case, as the history of probably every mining district in England proves. Here is testimony upon the point, taken at random:—

"In 1885 a company in West Cumberland had eight blast furnaces, four of which were idle, not because the firm had no work, but simply owing to the high royalty demanded by the landowner. The company applied, but unsuccessfully, for a reduction; and, in order to fulfil their contracts with the Indian Government, the firm had to import iron from Belgium, while at the same time half their furnaces, and consequently half their workmen, were idle. A blast furnace turns out about 600 tons of pig iron per week, and upon these 600 tons the royalties amounted to £202, while the wages paid to everyone engaged in producing these 600 tons, from manager downwards, amounted to only £95. Failing to obtain a reduction in the royalty demanded, the

---

Parliament. It is closely connected with the question of royalties, which is now being considered by a Royal Commission. As the law stands at present, if the search for coal be successful, the neighbouring landowners, who may or may not have contributed to the experiment, are masters of the situation, because they can charge what royalties they like."

[1] The number of workpeople employed in and at mines in the United Kingdom is estimated at 600,000, and to these come another 600,000 for iron and steel works.

company purchased land in America, transferred their works, and are now numbered amongst our foreign competitors."[1]

And again, in an address delivered in Glasgow in 1885, Mr. Forsyth, president of the Scottish Land Restoration League, said:—

"Out of eighty blast furnaces in Cumberland forty are at this moment standing idle, and the others are but partially employed. There are many causes which might have the effect of keeping these forty blast furnaces idle. They might be idle for want of capital; they might be idle for want of men willing to work; but the Cumberland furnaces are put out, not because of any lack of capital, for only within the last week or two a company of employers there were willing to sink £20,000 in raising iron ore, and were only prevented from doing so by the landlord's ultimatum that he would not reduce his royalty of 2s. 6d. per ton on the ore which might be raised. The company found that with this charge they could not raise ore as cheaply as it could be imported from Spain, and they therefore abandoned their project. Neither can it be that there are not men able and willing to work, for an ironmaster in Cumberland writes saying that there are thousands of men unemployed who would be glad to find work of any kind in order to save their wives and children from starvation."

In a pamphlet by Mr. C. M. Percy, Wigan, "Mine Rents and Mineral Royalties," mention is made of a case in which—

"In 1869 a lease was granted for a term extending until 1894, at a fixed certain minimum royalty which had to be paid whether any coal was wanted or not, and if any more coal was got than

---

[1] Mr. R. M'Ghee, in an address to the Govan (Glasgow) Liberal Association (quoted in the "Financial Reform Almanack" for 1890).

the minimum grant represented, all that additional quantity paid additional royalty. The tenant expended £50,000, and in 1875 asked the consent of the landlord to the transfer of his lease. The landlord demanded a fine amounting to ten years' rent, and ultimately accepted a fine equal to five years' rent. In 1877 the lease was again transferred, and the landlord made a further demand of a fine amounting to five years' rent, and ultimately accepted a fine equal to three years' rent."

Again, in the same work, as to Cornwall:—

"Leases are granted usually for twenty-one years. There are heavy fixed rates and dues on the output, paid in many cases not from profits but from actual calls on shareholders, the mines themselves being worked at a loss. Enormous charges are made for surface damage to land, as much as £100 per acre of land whose annual value is £1. At the expiration of the lease the entire plant becomes the property of the landlord. . . The tenant gets nothing for 'unexhausted improvements' which his money has made."

Not only is the mining monopoly at present possessed by the landowners a public danger, whether regarded from the standpoint of the capitalist who floats or the labourer who works mines, but the effect of this monopoly, involving as it does the levying of an inordinate tribute upon industrial enterprise, is to make minerals and their products cost far more to the consumer than should be the case. I lay no stress whatever upon the obstacle thus placed in the way of the export of minerals, regarding it as an advantage rather than otherwise that the natural wealth of the country stored in mines—and especially coal—should be conserved for home use, instead of being sent abroad, often at absolutely insignificant profit to the producer.[1]

Much injustice is, however, suffered by home consumers, who have a right to the fullest possible benefit from the minerals with which the country is blessed. This they can only have when the principle for which I am contending is applied to mineral-containing land, equally with the land which is built upon and the land which is merely cultivated. Future increase of value to land from the development of existing mines or the discovery of new ones should not be appropriated by the owners of the soil, since that increase is due to no merit or service or exertion on their part, but to the bountifulness of the Creator who bestowed upon us the minerals and to the society whose needs give them value.[2]

---

[1] The coal supplies of Great Britain are being depleted to the extent of millions of tons yearly for the benefit of foreign countries, for it is well known that the gain on export is very small. The coal output of the United Kingdom for the years 1880-4 amounted to 782 million tons, and we exported during those years about 100 million tons at an average price of 9s. per ton. Our coalfields are limited in extent, yet of vast importance for our future industrial prosperity. Why should we thus drain them so cheaply?

[2] In Austria the landlords have no exclusive claim to the minerals beneath the surface. "Anybody who takes out a search licence is entitled to search for minerals on anybody's property. The proprietor has, of course, to be indemnified; but, if he be unreasonable in his demands, the searcher can obtain a compulsory lease, or sale at a valuation price, of the ground which he requires for sinking a pit or borehole."

Writing in September, 1890, a *Times* correspondent in Vienna says:—"This system has done wonders in Austria, and one may safely say that without it the Austrian mining industry would never have attracted so much foreign capital and attained to its present flourishing state."

CHAPTER X.

HALF-REMEDIES.

IF it be granted that the community can properly claim that social value in land which has been created by causes operating independently of the owners, the more serious question arises: How shall the claim be made good? There are those who regard this practical phase of the subject as in reality very unpractical. Even so clear-sighted a man as Mr. John Bright once declared[1] Mill's proposal that the State should appropriate a portion of the unearned increment to be "so absolutely impracticable" as to be unworthy of discussion. But are the difficulties in the way so very great as to be insuperable?

Here it is desirable to refer to two plans which have been recommended as offering at least a tentative solution of the problem. One is the purchase by towns of the fee-simple of their districts. By this arrangement the land upon which a town is built would belong to the local community as a whole, the

---

[1] January, 1884.

buildings alone to the inhabitants or other individual owners, and all future increased value would be a common possession.[1] This proposal, which has many supporters, especially amongst those who aim at the nationalisation of the land—to which goal it is a halfway house—has attained greater prominence in England since Mr. E. D. Gray, M.P., developed it in a memorandum appended to the first report of the Commission on the Housing of the Working Classes.

"The only thorough remedy," wrote Mr. Gray, "is to enable the local authority in every town (agricultural land must be considered separately) to acquire the fee-simple of the entire of its district compulsorily, and for this purpose the district should be so enlarged as to include the probable growth of the town for a considerable period. This proposition may appear extravagant, but in principle it is a mere extension of the provisions of Sir Richard Cross's Acts. Those Acts enable a sanitary authority to purchase an 'area' compulsorily, and to take premises not in themselves in an unsanitary condition, if requisite to make the 'scheme' complete. The principle of taking property compulsorily for the benefit of the working classes, even when the individual owner has been guilty of no default, is thus fully recognised. If it is just thus to take one man's property, it is just to take many men's property under the same conditions if

---

[1] Over thirty years ago Professor F. W. Newman, in his "Lectures on Political Economy" (published 1857) said:—"In the centre of a trading town . . . we cannot murmur against the existence of ground-rent, however high, but only at the scandal of its having been wantonly granted away to private persons, instead of reserving it by law as a town property. When the use of the land is manifestly essential to the life of the community, it is an obvious maxim of political justice that the rent should be limited by law. . . The land on which a town is built ought never to be held in masses by a small number of persons."

the public interest requires it. It is now simply proposed to make the 'area' extend to the whole 'district,' for in no other way can the 'scheme' be made really complete and of permanent benefit. The community, represented by the local authority, would then have the benefit of such future increase in the value of the land of the town as was due to its increased prosperity, caused either by the industry and enterprise of the community, or to circumstances equally beyond its control, and that of the original fee-simple holders of the land. Such a change, while inflicting no injustice upon any individual, provided a fair purchase price were paid, would, in consequence of the future enhanced value of the land, eventually not only do away with the necessity of local taxation in towns, but yield a constantly increasing surplus applicable to the benefit of the entire community. . . . . The local authority would let the land at its disposal on conditions favourable to the development and protection of building enterprise by giving full security to those who invested their money or their labour thereon, while the profit and future 'unearned increment' would go to the community."

While this plan has nowhere in England been adopted in its entirety, there are nevertheless many towns whose corporations own considerable areas which they lease to advantage for building purposes, thus securing on reversion the increase of value. To such towns the report of the Committee on Town Holdings alludes:—

"It appears to be sometimes urged that any large increase of land-values during the currency of building leases is not in fact an unearned increment, but is due to the general industry and prosperity of the community. The fallacy of this argument as used for the purpose of justifying the expropriation of the freeholders by the lessees lies in confounding together the lessees and the community. As has been already stated, the evidence shows that the lessees are not the community, but only a very small fraction of it. And there is neither reason nor justice in assigning to a small section that which is due to the exertions of the general body. The distinction is clearly shown in cases where the Corporation of a town, as at Waterford, Dublin,[1] Liverpool, Birmingham, or Nottingham, hold, as trustees for the community, land which they let upon building-lease. By such a process the increase of land-values, which is due, not to the building that has taken place, but to the localised industry and general prosperity of the whole body of citizens, seems, according to the evidence, to be most satisfactorily secured for the general benefit of those to whom it is due."

This plan is not peculiar to English social reformers. It forms a part of the programme to which many of the leading State Socialists of Germany have committed themselves. Professor Wagner, of Berlin, advocated it years ago in his earlier works on political economy.[2] He, in fact, asks for the entire abolition of private property in residential land. In towns there should be collective possession of both land and houses, the communities buying the former and building the latter. It is worthy of note, too, that twenty years ago a similar scheme was advocated by the more moderate section of the Social-Democratic party in Germany. A useful object-lesson may, indeed, be taken from that

---

[1] In the year 1881 an amount of property belonging to the Dublin Corporation fell out of lease—the lease having been made in 1682—and the result was that a largely increased rental fell to the city, the leap being from £36 4s. to £2,000.

[2] See the *Grundlegung* to his "*Lehrbuch der politischen Oekonomie*" (Leipzig, 1876), chapter v., sec. 354 *et seq.*

country. When Prussia annexed Hanover, after the war of 1866, she still retained the " domains" in fiscal hands. These lands were revalued, and as a result rents, which had hitherto been far too low, were advanced from 40 to 120 per cent., the State thus deriving the benefit.

A significant move in the same direction was (theoretically) made by our own House of Commons when, on May 6th last, it adopted, by 175 votes against 159, the following resolution :—

"That in the opinion of this House a measure is urgently needed enabling Town Councils and County Councils in England to acquire by agreement or compulsorily, on fair terms and by simple and inexpensive machinery, such land within or adjoining their several districts as may in their judgment be needed for the requirements of the inhabitants."

Yet, however admirable this proposal in its intention, and however beneficial to the extent of its application, it cannot be denied that it is after all an imperfect and incomplete plan. The unearned increment problem would be solved so far as the towns were concerned, but agricultural land—in fact, all non-residential land—and mines would be untouched. At the best, therefore, there could be no finality about such a measure. Society would still suffer injustice, the same in character if not equal in extent.

Again, great interest has of late been aroused in England in what is known as the "Betterment" principle. We have already seen how the public improvements carried on in towns frequently increase the value of the property they adjoin to an enormous degree. The advocates of the betterment principle would allow the owners of such property to retain the increment so created, though they would take away its unearned character by throwing a portion of the cost of an improvement upon the persons financially benefited. The betterment tax, as Mr. John Rae[1] shows, has been known in America for nearly two centuries. He tells us :—

"The power to impose such an assessment was given to a Highway Board in the county of Ulster, in the colony of New York, in the year 1691, for the purpose of making public roads, and the same power was again given the same year to the Corporation of the city of New York for the construction of the public streets. These Acts were still in force in 1773, when Von Schaack published his collection of statutes, and their betterment clauses were re-affirmed in 1787, when the old colonial statutes were revised for the new State constitution under the Republic. As the city grew, fresh Improvement Acts were required, and the same provision of a betterment tax for the partial or total payment of the expense incurred by the improvements was contained in the successive Acts of 1793, 1795, 1796, 1801, and 1813. The betterment tax therefore originated in the very infancy of New York, and has continued ever since one of the ordinary ways and means of meeting the cost of city improvements. It was a common custom there even before it was sanctioned by any statute. When the city fathers dug a new

---

[1] Article in the *Contemporary Review* for May, 1890, on "The Betterment Tax in America."

well they always laid half the expense on the city generally, and the other half on the owners of the property nearest to the well. That was done in the case of public wells in Broadway, Pearl Street, and other parts in 1676."

Though the betterment principle set root in New York State so long ago, its introduction into the other States of the North American Union is of much more recent date; in fact, belonging to the last half-century. Thus the principle has only been in operation in Boston since 1866, having been introduced in the city's Improvement Act of that year, yet by its instrumentality many public improvements, costing large sums of money, have been carried out at moderate cost to the ratepayers. So accustomed now are the communities of the States to this tax that "for the last ten years there seems almost an entire absence of litigation[1] against this form of impost;" and, in the words of a judge of the Supreme Court of Missouri, "it is now as firmly established as any other doctrine of American law."

---

[1] A case is related where, owing to the operation of the betterment principle, a New York landowner, part of whose land was taken for public improvements, was called on to pay a sum of money into the bargain on account of the increased value given to the rest of his estate. "He flew to law but was told that he could claim no damages for sustaining a benefit. 'The owner of property taken,' said the Chancellor, 'is entitled to a full compensation for the damage he sustained thereby, but if the taking of his property for a public improvement is a benefit rather than an injury to him, he certainly has no equitable claim of damages.' And the Chancellor's view was confirmed on appeal by a unanimous judgment in the Court for Correction of Errors." (Related by Mr. J. Rae in the *Contemporary Review* for May, 1890.)

In England no general law specifically incorporating the betterment principle has ever existed. Here the strange anomaly still exists that while local authorities may be compelled to pay compensation for injury caused to the property of individuals by reason of the measures they adopt in the public interest—as in the erection of public buildings, as schools, the diversion of a road, or the like—they cannot claim indemnity from the persons whose property their expenditure on improvements may benefit.[1] Partial acknowledgment of this principle was, however, secured earlier in England than in America.

---

[1] Thus, before the County of London Sheriff's Court on January 3rd, 1890, a licensed victualler and leasehold occupier of a public house in Clerkenwell Road "claimed compensation from the London County Council for injury to his interest in the premises in question, consequent upon diversion of traffic and trade caused by the Council's improvements in connection with the construction of the new road known as Rosebery Avenue. The amount entered in the formal claim was £3,000." The claim was non-suited, as it was found that damage had not been sustained, but the Council's counsel admitted that "if there had been deterioration in the value of the property in consequence of the action of the County Council a legal claim for compensation could have been sustained."

Mr. Charles Harrison, in a letter to the *Times*, January 8th, 1890, mentions the following case, in which the owner of a public-house near Old Putney Bridge obtained damages: "The Metropolitan Board of Works built a new bridge [to replace the old Putney Bridge] a short distance up the river, but executed no new works in the main street in which the public-house was situated. The Board made a new thoroughfare joining the old main-street; the traffic which formerly went along the main street past the public-house subsequently passed along the new thoroughfare and so over the new bridge. The publican claimed and obtained from the jury £1,031 compensation solely on account of the diversion of traffic."

The first English law in which the principle is asserted is the Sewers Act of 1427 (6 Henry VI.), amended in 1531 by Act of 23 Henry VIII., the Statute of Sewers now in force. By these laws Commissioners of Sewers were appointed and the works executed under their direction were charged upon the lands directly benefited.[1] Then, again, in the Act of 19 Charles II., c. 2, for the rebuilding of the City of London after the Great Fire of 1666, the principle is clearly laid down.[2] Coming to quite recent times the Artisans' Dwellings Acts of 1879 and 1882[3] recognise the justice of the

[1] The preamble of the earlier statute states that "considering the great damage and losses which now late be happened by the great inundation of waters in divers parts of the realm, and that much greater damage is very like to ensue if remedy be not speedily provided," "several Commissions of Sewers shall be made to divers persons by the Chancellor of England for the time being, to be sent into all parts of the realm where shall be needful."

[2] After making provision for the enlargement and widening of various old streets and passages, the Act proceeds (section 24):— "And forasmuch as the houses now remaining and to be rebuilt will receive more or less advantage in the value of their rents by the liberty of air and free recourse of trade, and other conveniences by such regulation and enlargement, it is also enacted by the authority aforesaid that, in case of refusal or incapacity as aforesaid of the owners or others interested of or in the said houses to agree and compound with the said Lord Mayor, Aldermen, and Commons for the same: Thereupon a jury shall and may be impanelled in manner and form aforesaid, to judge and assess upon the owners and others interested of and in such houses, such competent sum and sums of money with respect to their several interests, in consideration of such improvement and melioration, as in reason and good conscience shall think fit. . . And the money so raised shall be wholly employed towards payment and satisfaction of such houses and ground as shall be converted into streets, passages, markets, and other public places aforesaid."

[3] Before this, various attempts were made to resuscitate the betterment principle. A quarter of a century ago (in 1866) the

principle. In the former measure it is provided that in the fixing of the compensation payable to an owner on account of the demolition of his property, regard shall be had to any additional value thus given to the adjoining property of the same owner. The Act of 1882 goes further, for it provides that where an obstructive building[1] is taken for the purpose of improving the adjacent property, the improvement given to that property may be charged upon it in the form of a rate in aid.[2] The betterment provisions of these two

---

Select Committee on Metropolitan Government recommended the levy of a tax on owners in aid of the cost of permanent improvements made in London. The same principle underlay the proposal of the Select Committee upon Local Taxation, which, under the presidency of Mr. Goschen, recommended in 1870 that occupiers should be entitled to throw part of the rates upon the landlords by deducting it from the rent.

[1] In the Housing of the Working Classes (Amendment) Bill of 1890 an "obstructive building" is defined as "a building so situate that by reason of its proximity to or contact with other buildings it (among other things) prevents proper measures from being carried into effect for remedying the evils complained of in respect of such other buildings" (the "evils complained of" including nuisances injurious to health).

[2] The exact wording of section 8 of this Act is as follows:— "Where, in the opinion of the arbitrator, the demolition of an *obstructive building* adds to the value of such other buildings as are in that behalf mentioned in this section, the arbitrator shall apportion so much of the compensation to be paid for the demolition of the obstructive building as may be equal to the increase in the value of the other buildings amongst such other buildings respectively, and the amount apportioned to each such other building in respect of its increase in value by reason of the demolition of such obstructive building shall be deemed to be private improvement expenses," &c.

These "private improvement expenses" fall largely upon the occupier. Sir Hugh Owen, Permanent Secretary of the Local Government Board, stated before the Commission on the Housing of the Working Classes:—"A private improvement rate is borne to

measures were rendered necessary by the difficulty which always accompanied the removal of old property by improving communities owing to the extortionate compensation demanded and secured by adjacent landowners. The report of the Commission on the Housing of the Working Classes says :—

"The evidence has shown that there have been striking instances of compensation which has been paid in cases where persons have received payment for actual advantage which has accrued to their property from the demolitions or alterations; for example, where a portion of property is taken in order to widen a street. It was stated by Mr. Chamberlain that enormous compensations have been paid to landowners in such cases. Six feet, for instance, has been taken off their frontage, and instead of facing, as they have hitherto done, a mean court or a wretched side street, they find themselves on a great thoroughfare, and the remaining part of their property is worth twice or three times as much as the whole of it was worth before; and yet, although nothing is taken from them by way of contribution, they may have secured enormous compensation."

During the last few months the subject has been much discussed in and out of Parliament by reason of the promotion by the London County Council of a Bill —unfortunately wrecked—containing clauses intended to legalise the betterment tax in respect of the contemplated widening of the Strand.[1] Section 28 of the Strand Improvement Bill said :—

some extent by the occupier of the premises, and I hardly think it quite fair that the occupier should be called upon to pay, in addition to his rent, for the improvement of the owner's property."

[1] "As a practical proof of Strand 'betterment' it may be mentioned that a public-house in that thoroughfare, which three years

"And whereas the improvement, being effected out of public funds belonging to or charged upon the ratepayers of the county of London, will or may increase in value lands or property fronting on or in the neighbourhood of the improvement, but not acquired for the purpose thereof, and it is reasonable that provision should be made under which such increased value should be reserved wholly or in part for the ratepayers at whose expenditure it has been produced, therefore: (1) There shall be a rent charge, to be called the Strand Improvement Rent Charge, which shall be fixed, ascertained, charged, and payable in manner hereinafter described; but the total of the Strand Improvement Rent Charge shall not be of any amount which, when capitalised on such basis as the Standing Arbitrator may deem reasonable, would in his opinion exceed one half of the cost of the improvement," &c.

Yet here, again, while the aim of the friends of the betterment principle is laudable, and while that principle is perfectly just and equitable, the same objection holds good as in the case of purchasing the fee-simple of towns; we have not here a complete solution of the unearned increment problem.[1] The

---

ago was bought for £9,200, has just changed hands for £16,300!—and of course during the period in question very large annual profits were made."—*Daily Telegraph*, April, 1890.

[1] It is important to notice the opinions which have been expressed on this subject by leading Liberal statesmen. The views of Mr. Gladstone have already been referred to. Mr. J. Morley has spoken still more decisively. Addressing the members of the Eighty Club on November 19th, 1889, he spoke of "the monstrous iniquity that landlords whose property is enhanced in value, owing to expenditure to which they do not contribute, are allowed to pocket the enhancement of value," adding :—"It may last till 1899, but I do not think it will, but whether it does or not let us make up our minds what we are to tell to our constituents and to the audiences that we address in the country. Let us tell them that those who derive most of the permanent benefit of the en-

plan of levying improvement contributions on landlords only applies to one kind of increment, or, to speak with greater accuracy, to only one species of one genus. There is, as we saw at the outset, an *urban* increment (that created in the town) ; and there is a *rural* increment, in the production of which different causes operate. Moreover, taking the social value of town land, there is that value which is attributable directly to public improvements—and these only were contemplated by the London County Council—and there is the value which is due to the general progress of society, and it is in respect to this that the inadequacy of the betterment principle becomes especially apparent.

---

hanced value are those who contribute least to the expenditure that produced that enhancement. Let us go to those men and say to them, ' You shall not go on pocketing this increased value. You shall not go on taking permanent advantage and paying none of the costs. You shall bear a fair and a good share of the expenditure which produced that advantage.' Surely this is all plain common-sense and justice. We need not go into the metaphysics of land nationalisation, nor into absolute ethics or relative ethics. The plain common-sense of Englishmen will tell them that this is a system which ought now, without delay, to be peremptorily brought to an end."

CHAPTER XI.

ROOT AND BRANCH.

THERE can be no doubt that taxation is the most effectual means of getting at unearned increment—of "tapping" it for the benefit of society. By this plan it will be possible to gather the whole of the increment into the social net, thus allowing the community—represented by the State, the County Council, the municipality, the urban authority, or whatever organ may be considered the best for the purpose—for the future to keep its own. It may be said that property owners do already pay both higher taxes and higher rates because of the growing value of their possessions. But it is not enough merely to return to society in this way a low rate of interest on the value which it has created. Society has a right to the entire capital worth. To take an example: The value of a given quantity of land is to day £100; a later valuation shows it to be worth £120. This increase is demonstrably not due to any labour, any exertions, any expenditure of capital on the owner's part, but to purely social causes. The increment of £20 should not, then, be appropriated by the landlord, who has not done anything to create it, but by the community. Surely no real injustice would be inflicted upon a man by withholding from him something which he never possessed. This unearned increment never was his; how, therefore, could he be said to suffer injustice if society, without touching the orginal £100, kept all value exceeding that amount.

On this subject Mill (after premising that "there are cases in which exceptions may be made to" the principle of equality of taxation "consistently with that equal justice which is the groundwork of the rule") says forcibly:—

"Suppose that there is a kind of income which constantly tends to increase, without any exertion or sacrifice on the part of the owners: those owners constituting a class in the community whom the natural course of things progressively enriches, consistently with complete passiveness on their own part. In such a case it would be no violation of the principles on which private property is grounded, if the State should appropriate this increase of wealth, or part of it, as it arises. This would not properly be taking anything from anybody; it would merely be applying an accession of wealth, created by circumstances, to the benefit of society, instead of allowing it to become an unearned appendage to the riches of a particular class." [1]

Here it will be interesting to inquire how far Mill is really prepared to go. After asking what claim the

---

[1] "Principles of Political Economy," Book V., chap. ii., sec. 5.

landlords have, " on the general principle of social justice," to the increase of riches which is caused by society's progress, he proceeds :—

"In what would they have been wronged if society had from the beginning reserved the right of taxing the spontaneous increase of rent to the highest amount required by financial exigencies? I admit that it would be unjust to come upon each individual estate, and lay hold of the increase which might be found to have taken place in its rental; because there would be no means of distinguishing between an increase owing to the general circumstances of society, and one which was the effect of skill and expenditure on the part of the proprietor. The only admissible mode of proceeding would be by a general measure. The first step should be a valuation of all the land in the country. The present value of all land should be exempt from the tax; but after an interval had elapsed, during which society had increased in population and capital, a rough estimate might be made of the spontaneous increase which had accrued to rent since the valuation was made. Of this the average price of produce would be some criterion; if that had risen it would be certain that rent had increased, and even in a greater ratio than the rise of price. On this and other data an approximate estimate might be made how much value had been added to the land of the country by natural causes; and in the laying on a general land tax, which for fear of miscalculation should be considerably within the amount thus indicated, there would be an assurance of not touching any increase of income which might be the result of capital expended or industry exerted by the proprietor. . . From the present date or any subsequent time at which the Legislature may think fit to assert the principle, I see no objection to declaring that the future increment of rent should be liable to special taxation; in doing which all injustice to the landlords would be obviated if the present market-price of their land were secured to them; since that includes the present value of all future expectations. With reference to such a tax, perhaps a safer criterion than either a rise of rents or a rise of the price of corn would be a general rise in the price of land. It would be easy to keep the tax within the amount which would reduce the market-value of land below the original valuation; and up to that point, whatever the amount of the tax might be, no injustice would be done to the proprietors." [1]

The two principal objections to Mill's proposal of a general uniform land tax are, (1) that it would only afford society partial relief and protection for the future, and (2) that the incidence of this tax would be very unequal. The first of these objections needs no further amplification. As to the second, it must be evident that if land of all kinds, and in all parts of the country, were to be placed in one category, neither society as a whole nor individual landowners would be certain of receiving justice. In a country in which, as in England, agriculture is divided between the two great branches of corn-growing and grazing, it is quite possible that there may be considerable variation in the *relative* values of land applied to such different purposes. It is a fact that, during the agricultural crisis of the past few years, Southern farmers touched a far lower level of depression than farmers in many parts of the North; and even amongst corn growers as a class, and graziers as a class, there was much variety of circumstances and fortune. Again, agricultural land differs considerably in value and

---

[1] "Principles of Political Economy," Book V., chap., ii. sec. 5.

in augmentation of value according to location. The land adjacent to towns increases in value more rapidly than that which lies where population is sparse. What, then, would be the effect of the imposition of a uniform land tax by reason of a " general rise in the price of land ? " The landowners of industrial districts would feel it no hardship to pay the tribute levied on the increment which had accrued to them, but others might find the burden unjust, because disproportionate to the increased value of their lands. The only way of avoiding this inequality is to "come upon each individual estate," and this plan Mill does not recommend.

But the greatest objection to be raised against Mill's proposal of a uniform increment tax arises out of the utterly different position of urban and agricultural land. Where agricultural land may, in a given period, increase in value one per cent., the land upon which towns are built may—and, probably, often does—increase a hundred per cent. Indeed, speaking generally, urban land is perpetually increasing in value, but this cannot be said of agricultural land. While the cloud of depression was hanging heaviest over the farming industry of England, and holdings might be bought at figures lower than for many years, land in our large towns continued without cessation to rise in value. It follows, therefore, that a tax fairly representing society's claim on the increment which had accrued to agricultural land might be an utterly and absurdly inadequate proportion of the increment created in towns.

It seems to me that the most effective and the only equitable solution of the difficulty would be found if the plan to which Mill objects were adopted, and we "came upon each individual estate [urban and rural alike] and laid hold of the increase which might be found to have taken place in its rental." Mill's argument against this plan is that "there would be no means of distinguishing, in individual cases, between an increase owing solely to the general circumstances of society, and one which was the effect of skill and expenditure on the part of the proprietor." In reply it may be admitted that all expenditure which tended to the permanent improvement of land ought to be regarded as a set-off against the increase in its capital value, and to this extent society should have no claim upon the increment caused. For example, if a landlord went to expense in improving an agricultural holding, by draining the land and placing buildings upon it, there should be no claim upon the increment found on re-valuation to have been created, so long as that increment was not out of proportion to the additional investment of capital in the land. If, on the other hand, that increment were, for evident reasons, so large as to be disproportionate to the capital expended in the permanent improvement of the holding, the excess of increment due to causes acting independently of the owner should go to society.¹

It seems probable that the question would best be settled in conjunction with the re-adjustment of the land tax. This tax, as is well known, is now very insignificant in its return, and very irregular and unjust in its incidence.² The last statute which

---

¹ The views here expounded receive partial acceptance from M. Emile de Laveleye, who, writing on the increase in land-values in Belgium since 1830 (*vide* the Cobden Club's "Systems of Land Tenure in various Countries," edition 1881, p. 467), says :—"Part of this progressive increase in rent may be traced to improvements made by the farmer in the cultivation of the soil. By raising the rent the landlord lays hold for himself of this advance in the value of the land produced by those who cultivate it. The increase of the revenue the landlord derives from his land is not the result of improvements executed by himself, and the fact adverted to is a general one, which may be met with everywhere. In whatever cases landlords have actually made improvements, they have got the interest of the outlay in the shape of an additional augmentation of their revenue. For these reasons (he adds) I think that the increase of rent, being due to the progress of society at large, and not to the exertions of the landowners, ought not in justice to benefit the latter alone. It would be but fair to divide this benefit."

² "In most countries of Europe the right to take by taxation, as exigency might require, an indefinite portion of the rent of land has never been allowed to slumber. In several parts of the Continent the land tax forms a large proportion of the public revenues, and has *always been confessedly liable to be raised or lowered without reference to other taxes*. . . . In England the land tax has not varied since the early part of the last century." (Mill's "Principles of Political Economy," Book V., chap. ii., sec. 5.)

"In most countries a tax on the rent of land forms a notable item in the revenue receipts. In the United Kingdom it is included in the income tax, the so-called land tax being a rent issuing from

ROOT AND BRANCH. 147

regulated the tax was passed in 1798. The Act imposed a fixed tax, payable by each parish in perpetuity, subject to the option of redemption.[1] The rate was 4s. in the pound, and the tax then yielded about two million pounds. Redemptions have reduced the yield to about a million pounds, a sum which is very unequally raised. As the quotas payable by the parishes were made invariable, strange anomalies have arisen. Where population has greatly increased, and the value of land has proportionately risen, the rate per pound has fallen to a totally inadequate sum. No parish now pays the full original rate of 4s. in the pound, but there are many parishes which pay only 1d. in the

---

the land, invariable, redeemable, and wholly disproportionate to the present value of the property from which it is derived." (Professor Thorold Rogers, "Political Economy," chap. xxii.)

Mr. Goschen said in his report to the House of Commons on Local Taxation, August 10th, 1870 :—" The amount paid by land alone towards imperial taxation in England is five and a-half per cent. ; in Holland nine per cent. ; in Austria seventeen and a-half per cent. ; in France eighteen and a-half per cent. ; in Belgium twenty and a-half per cent. ; and in Hungary thirty-two and a-half per cent. What do these facts prove? They prove that, as regards imperial taxation, land in this country is in an infinitely better position than land in any other European State."

[1] The effect of Pitt's Land Tax Redemption Act—which was but a money-making expedient—was to perpetuate the land tax at its then height. The valuation was that of 1692, made under William III., in accordance with a statute providing "that an aid be granted to His Majesty of 4s. in the pound on the true yearly value of real property and on all salaries," &c. The assessment on the land realised £2,037,627, and in 1697 Parliament fixed two millions as the future limit of the land tax. Pitt's Act made this levy perpetual.

L 2

pound, and the rate of some is as low as a hundredth of a penny.

This tax should, as a preliminary step towards its complete re-adjustment, be redeemed on easy terms. When it had been swept away the deck would be clear for the introduction of a new and rational land tax. A general valuation would be necessary for the purpose, and this made, an equitable tax should be imposed—so much in the pound, applying to urban and rural land equally. For the future, however, there should be valuations at definite intervals—say, every five years for town land, and at longer periods for agricultural land—in order to learn the increase in value, if any. After the first re-valuation and after every succeeding valuation a *special tax* should be levied upon that increase in the rental which could be shown to be due to social causes. The amount of the original valuation, together with any increase attributable to the owner's expenditure or exertions, would only be subject to the general land tax, but the amount beyond that, as it represented society's contribution to the value of the land, should belong to the community.

Whether unearned increment socially appropriated should go to the State or to the local communities is a secondary question, though much may be said in favour of each local government district retaining the whole of the additional value which its population may have given to the land it uses. The freeholder or leaseholder, as the case might be, should pay over the increment to society in the form of taxation. For various reasons it would not be desirable to require the payment of its capital value in a lump sum. In the first place, such a plan would often entail hardship, as it would compel many owners to borrow or sell part of their property in order to liquidate their indebtedness. But a more serious, and indeed fatal, objection lies in the fact that owners are often, by agreements of various kinds, precluded from present participation in the increasing value of their land. On the one hand it would not be just to expect a landlord so circumstanced to pay down the capital value of an increment of which he does not enjoy the benefit; but on the other hand it would be equally unfair to ask a temporary beneficiary to do this, as his interest in it would often be of short duration. It would not, however, be inequitable to impose such an annual tax as would absorb the whole of the increased rental falling to the landlord in consequence of the increment socially created. This tax would represent the landowner's payment to society in consideration of its proprietary interest in the land.

To show how this plan would work in two directions —applied to town and also agricultural land.

(1.) Let us, first, for the sake of argument, suppose the present value of an urban property to be £1,000, yielding a rental of £50. The landlord would pay upon the value of the land (apart from buildings) the initial and uniform land tax to be fixed. After a certain number of years a re-valuation is made, and it is found that the property is worth £1,200, and that the rental is £60. In the absence of expenditure by the landlord for the improvement of the property the spontaneous increase will be more than £200 (£10 rental), since the buildings will have depreciated in value.[1] When the actual value of the land alone had been determined, the increment would be recovered in the form of a special tax, to be modified or increased according as the next revision showed a diminution or a further growth in the value of the land. The depreciation of a building could not, of course, be allowed to prejudice society's claim to all the increment it might give to the land upon which that building stands, since in fixing the rent upon any structure a landlord has regard to its probable duration, and the tenant pays every year at once interest and depreciation.

(2.) In the case of purely agricultural land, the mode of procedure would be much simpler. Until a re-valuation took place the landlords would pay the uniform tax. Suppose during the interval an estate increased in

---

[1] So the report of the Committee on Town Holdings says :—" The decrease during the term of a 99 years' lease of the value of a house seems as a rule to be accompanied by a corresponding increase in the value of the land on which it stands."

value to the same extent as in the first illustration, from £1,000 to £1,200, and the rental from £50 to £60. Due allowance would be made for the quota attributable to the landlord's expenditure, and the remainder of the increment (if any) would be claimable in the way of special taxation.

But should society claim a share in any increment which evidently exists, even though not expressed in the form of increased rent? In order to err on the side of leniency it should not. So long as agricultural land did not return a higher rent owing to the tenant's exertions or social causes, society would be suffering no injury, and it would therefore be equitable to allow the initial tax to remain unincreased. In this respect, however, land built upon and land not so employed stand upon a different footing. Land is not subject to dilapidation and eventual decay as buildings are, and, as has been shown, a rise in the value and rent of a house-site is perfectly compatible with the absence of any increase in the value and rent of house and site together.

It follows as a matter of course, however, that on property changing hands either the increased social value which has accrued since the original valuation would be claimed in a lump sum by the community, or the property would be sold subject to a special tax large enough to absorb the return claimable upon that increased value. In other words, the owner would only receive the prime value *plus* such value as had been caused by his own improvements.

Should land be unused, not because the owner refused to let or sell on favourable terms, but from the absence of tenant or purchaser, some degree of relief from taxation might be considered equitable. There would no longer, however, be any inducement to withhold land from use because of the expectation of increasing value—a practice at present common in large towns, and one encouraged by existing rating law in England—for marketable land would invariably be returning rent. If it did not, society would be effectively protected by the local taxation of such land upon its full value.

But, it may be asked, if the maximum value (to the landlord) of land be fixed, as it practically would by this arrangement, should not that maximum be secured to the owner? If we determine that social causes shall not henceforth create for the landlords a higher value than their land at present possesses, is it not fair to guarantee them at least the existing value? If they may not gain in the future, should they not be protected against eventual loss? At present they take the good with the bad. If land-values increase at one time, they may fall at another; yet the owners do not permanently suffer, for a turn of fortune brings them recompense for their losses. Is not that plan, it may be argued, inequitable which exposes the landlords to risk, while not affording them an opportunity of recouping themselves for the sacrifices which the vicissitudes of industry and trade and other causes may sooner or later entail? As society is to benefit by all future increment, should not a minimum value be secured to all land? Those who pursue this line of argument overlook the vital fact that land entirely owes its value to human labour, in one form or other, and to the presence of population. Society originally gave value to the soil by dwelling upon it and by cultivating it; and even now, human need and use is the greatest factor in the value of land. Value may, therefore, be said to exist by the sufferance of society. There cannot be such a thing as a vested interest in the value of land. Did individuals or communities not require, for their own convenience, the land upon which they dwell and labour, it would not be worth more to the owners than such value as might represent the satisfaction of their own needs, desires, and purposes. To ask that a certain value may be assured to the landlords is to recognise an absolute obligation on the part of society as a whole to use, and pay for the use of, those portions of the earth's surface which certain of its members have been pleased to claim as their own. No such obligation exists.

It may be said that such a system of taxation as is

here advocated is complicated and would involve great difficulties. Granted; but the issues at stake are infinitely greater than any difficulties which might have to be faced. The machinery necessary, too, would be costly. True, but the proceeds of taxation would be enormous, and would afford society incalculable relief. Neither difficulty nor cost can be held to be a valid objection. Such fiscal institutions as the income tax, customs and excise, and local assessment were probably regarded as impracticable at one time or another, yet in spite of their intricate character they are found, after experiment, to be eminently workable. Surely the genius and sagacity which have caused our present fiscal machinery to move with at least tolerable smoothness would not find in the imposition of this new tax an insuperable problem. But with this as with all far-going reforms the difficulty lies more in the will than the way. Let public opinion call for the social appropriation of the unearned increment, and politicians and parties will vie for the credit of demonstrating that such appropriation is possible.

It is not too much to claim for this question the foremost place in the programme of urgent land-law reforms. Other phases of the land problem may, indeed, for evident reasons, be given a preferential position by those leaders of thought who believe that in dealing with the problem the reforming legislator will, in the future as in the past, be able to work with his hands in kid gloves. But sooner or later the question will have to be faced boldly, and it is very desirable that people should begin at once seriously to recognise its significance. There are few social questions the study of which does not bring us ultimately to the land, and generally that destination is reached very soon. Whatever class of people the reformers of to-day may seek to benefit and to elevate—be it the rack-rented and sweated toiler of the city, the husbandman who looks longingly back upon the better days of yore, or the agricultural labourer who weighs the possibilities of a manhood to which, from no fault of his own, he has so lately and so slowly attained—the final *crux*, the last and highest stone of stumbling, is the land.

Let us not deceive ourselves. Free land, the disintegration of *latifundia*, allotments, peasant proprietary, leasehold enfranchisement are all desirable and excellent so far as they go. But they will not settle the land question. So long as society is punished for its progress, so long as the fair fruits of civilisation, of enlightenment, of public enterprise, and individual exertion are appropriated by the landowners, it cannot be said that the gravity and deep significance of this question are comprehended. All the reforms enumerated are intended to benefit that part of the community which is directly associated with the land, and they would only benefit society in so far as every improvement in the welfare of the individual improves the welfare of the whole.

But the diversion of the unearned increment into public channels would be a measure of social benefit, for instead of being monopolised by the few who do *not* create it, it would be shared by the many who do. Such a distribution of the growing wealth of the community would not only be an act of social justice ; it would be productive of manifold positive blessings. Everywhere in town and country the pressure of taxation would be relieved. Industry and commerce would be emancipated from many harassing fetters. Honest enterprise would be encouraged. Men and women, born into a world already appropriated, destined here to live, would be able to breathe more freely. Society would henceforth labour to benefit, instead of to injure itself. In the factory, in the workshop, and by the plough, the busy sons of toil would labour more gladly, knowing that the wealth which they produced would fall in larger measure to themselves and to their children, affording comfort, leisure, and enjoyment now unknown. There would, in fine, be laid the foundations of a new and a higher social life, whose crowning characteristic and whose glory would be greater prosperity and happiness—greater and also truer, because more general.

PRINTED BY CHAS. STRAKER AND SONS, BISHOPSGATE AVENUE, LONDON, E.C.

INDEX.

AGRICULTURAL Holdings Acts, 113
Arnold, Mr. A., 5
America, land speculation in, 63-67
Artisans' Dwellings Acts, 86, 102
Austria, mineral rights in, 126

BELL, Sir I. L., on mineral royalties, 120
Brodrick, Hon. G. C., 5, 56
Broadhurst, M.P., Mr. H., 50, 51, 112
Berlin, value of land in, 19, 20, 67, 68, 95
Bright, Mr. John, 113, 127
Betterment principle, the, 131-139

CAIRNES, Professor J. E., 9
Chamberlain, Mr. J., 102
Compensation due to tenants for improvements, 45-48, 112, 116
Collings, M.P., Mr. J., 81
Compton, Earl, 87, 91

DEPRESSION in Trade and Industry, Royal Commission on, 60, 120, 121
Derby's property at Bury, the Earl of, 83, 84, 94, 95

ENGEL, Dr., 68, 81

FAWCETT, Professor, 4, 7
Fee-simple, purchase of urban, 127-129

GEORGE, Mr. Henry, 9, 58, 64, 70, 73, 119
Gladstone, Mr., 138
Goschen, Mr., 5, 36, 147
Gray, M.P., Mr. E. D., 128

HALLAM on land-values, testimony of, 2
Housing of the Working Classes, Commission on the, 72, 80, 84, 86, 91, 98, 99, 105, 137
Hill, Miss Octavia, 81

IRISH Land Acts, 113-116

LAND in the Middle Ages, value of, 2, 3
Land in modern times, value of, 3-10
Land in towns, value of, 6, 7, 13-39, 55-61
Land in London, value of, 6, 7, 15, 19
 ,, Berlin, 19, 20, 67, 68
 ,, Birmingham, 33-35
 ,, Dublin, 130
 ,, Burnley, 2
 ,, Bury, 14, 39
 ,, Germany, 5, 19, 20, 131
 ,, France, 5
 ,, Flanders, 5
 ,, Belgium, 5
 ,, San Francisco, 10, 58, 59, 70
 ,, New York, 10
 ,, United States, 7, 19, 58, 59, 65-67, 70, 119
 ,, Halifax, 33
Latimer, Hugh, on sixteenth century land-values, 7, 8
Land, price of, effect on wages of labour, 8-10
Land speculation, 30, 62-78
 ,, monopoly, the, 53-61, 70
 ,, dearness of, and poverty, 9, 10, 61
Land and overcrowding, 79-106
Local Taxation, Select Committee on, 36
Laveleye, M. E. de, 5, 146
Leasehold system, evils of, 42-52, 82, 84

INDEX.

Leasehold enfranchisement, 112
Life-leases, 49-52
Landowners in the United Kingdom, number of, 53, 54
Land Tax, the, 146

MILL, John Stuart, 37, 65, 109, 127, 141-146
Mines and mineral royalties, 117-126
Monopoly, the land, 14, 53-61, 70
Morley, Mr. John, 71, 111, 138

NEWMAN, Professor F. W., 128

O'CONNOR, M.P., Mr. A., 9, 60
Overcrowding in large towns, 79-106
Overcrowding and morality, 98-100

PEPYS' Diary, 32
Playfair, Sir Lyon, 6
Population, effect of on land-value and rent, 8, 22-24
Poverty and the land, 10
Public improvements, effect of on land-value, 24-39, 86, 103
Private gain at public cost, 22-52
Penalties of social progress, 1-10

RACK-RENTING in towns, 20, 21, 40-52, 69, 70, 81-103
Rae, Mr. John, 132, 133
Reap without sowing, how the landlords, 11-21
Rents in towns, high, 19-21, 40-52, 67-70, 81-103
Rogers, Professor Thorold, 2, 3, 7, 25, 57, 69, 102, 103, 109, 147
Rent screw, the, 40-52, 81-103, 114, 115
Railways, landowners and the, 5, 55, 59

Railways and land-values, 57-9
Rent and wages of workpeople, 88-93

SALISBURY, Lord, 105
Saunders, Mr. W., estimate of London land-values, 15, 87
Smith, Adam, 37, 38
Social progress and land-values, 1-21
Strand Improvement Bill, the, 30, 137-139
Speculation in land, 62-78, 103
Speculative building, 82-84

Taxation of ground values, 35-39, 71, 152
Taxation of unearned increment, 140-156
Town Holdings, evidence of Committee on, 18, 19, 23, 43-48, 62, 83, 112, 129, 150
Tenants, exploitation of, by landlords, 40-52

UNEARNED Increment, examples of, 6, 7, 14-24, 30-39, 119
Unearned Increment, how formed, 11-39
Unearned Increment, in towns, 13-52
Unearned Increment, in country, 11-14
Unearned Increment should go to society, 105-116, 140-156
United States, land-values in the, 7, 19, 58, 59, 65-67, 70, 119

YOUNG, Arth., on land-values, 3

WAGNER, Professor A., 30, 43, 44, 130
Wallace, Dr. A. R., 19, 63, 65
Webb, Mr. S., 15-18
Wages and rents of working people, 88-93

www.ingramcontent.com/pod-product-compliance
Lightning Source LLC
Chambersburg PA
CBHW030249170426
43202CB00009B/676